THE GREEN CORD DREAM

The Green Cord Dream

Pursuing Ellen White's Vision of Jesus and His Church

Alex Bryan

Pacific Press® Publishing Association
Nampa, Idaho
Oshawa, Ontario, Canada
www.pacificpress.com

Cover design by Gerald Lee Monks
Cover design resources from www.dreamstime.com
Inside design by Aaron Troia

You can obtain additional copies of this book by calling toll-free 1-800-765-6955 or by visiting http://www.adventistbookcenter.com.

Library of Congress Cataloging-in-Publication Data

Bryan, Alex, 1970–
Green cord dream : pursuing Ellen White's vision of Jesus and his church / Alex Bryan.
p. cm.
ISBN 13: 978-0-8163-2687-7 (pbk.)
ISBN 10: 0-8163-2687-8 (pbk.)
1. End of the world. 2. Seventh-day Adventists—Doctrines. 3. White, Ellen Gould Harmon, 1827–1915. I. Title.
BX6154.B79 2011
230'.6732—dc23

2011051385

12 13 14 15 16 • 5 4 3 2 1

Dedication

This book is dedicated to my wife, Nicole,
who models the compassionate love of Jesus
in our home, our church, and our community.

Contents

Chapter 1
The Green Cord Dream

The stream of Adventism is fed by the teardrops of the Great Disappointment.

We can't understand the currents of this faith movement, the flow of its theology, the rapids of its hopes and hang-ups, what floats it and at times drowns it, its eschatological energy, the life of its lifestyle, nor the refreshing river of its anthropological vision without an empathetic grasp of the October 22, 1844, punch in the gut.

It didn't happen on that day. He didn't appear. The clock struck midnight, and the Adventists were wrong. Tragically wrong. A whopper of a theological mistake. We argued from the Bible that the second coming of Jesus would happen on *this* date. We quit our jobs, left our homes, walked out of our churches. We sold our stuff. We looked to the sky. But there was no trumpet. There were no angels. There was no cloud.

The Advent movement was born in failure rather than

success, error rather than truth, darkness rather than light, and sorrow rather than joy.

Jesus didn't return.

The Great Disappointment.

Here is a truth: disappointments clarify, purging the streams of our lives of substances that might have clouded them. The disappointments of our lives bring sharper vision. They enable us to see who we are and what we are about. They make the hearts of men and women transparent.

In the fall of 1996, the Atlanta Braves, whom I adore, led the New York Yankees, whom I abhor, two games to one in the baseball World Series. At one point in game four, they held a six-run lead, and in the eighth inning they were still three runs ahead when Mark Wohlers, one of the Braves' better pitchers, threw a hanging slider—a very bad pitch. Jim Leyritz, the Yankee catcher, connected with that pitch, hitting a game-tying three-run homer over the left field wall. The Yankees won that game in extra innings, and they went on to win the World Series.

I'll bet you couldn't care less about the Braves' loss. It was fifteen years ago, and you might not even have lost two seconds of sleep that very night. Well, *I* did. I was so disappointed that I tossed, turned, and fidgeted, replaying that home run over and over again in my mind. And for days afterward, I talked with friends about the game: "Did you see what happened? Can you believe it?"

And now, a decade and a half later, I'm writing about it. In detail!

What does this reveal about me? That I've got some serious sports addiction issues? Whether healthy or not, this disappointment is clarifying. It says Alex Bryan loves baseball and the Atlanta Braves baseball team. It reveals me.

When she breaks up with you and you cry and you listen to sad songs on the radio and you write sappy poetry and you mope and you can't seem to cope, your disappointment reveals that you care deeply for *her.*

When you break up with her and ten minutes later she is shopping and fielding calls from other guys, happy and free, her lack of disappointment reveals what—or who—she doesn't care about. (Hint: *you.*)

When a son looks for his father in the stands, a father who fails to show up for his son's basketball game, the look of disappointment speaks.

When a daughter looks for her mother in the audience, a mother who fails to show up for her daughter's violin concert, the look of disappointment speaks.

These looks say, "I care about my girlfriend's/boyfriend's/parents' approval, love, affection, participation, presence in my life. I'm disappointed when they're absent because *I care about them and what they think about me.*"

One day I'll find the emotional courage to tell the full story of Nicole's and my years-long struggle with infertility. We couldn't have children. We spent big money on cutting-edge medical experimentation, but our baby dreams rested on techniques that just wouldn't work. I'll never forget hearing a good scientist with a horrible bedside manner tell my wife and me in a surgical recovery room, "I'm sorry. There's nothing there, and there never will be. You won't have children. You need to move on." The look on my wife's face: crushing disappointment. And I'm sure the look on my face revealed that my heart was shredded too.

We were humans who desperately wanted to become parents. It was our sorrow that pulled back the curtain that covered the deepest places of the soul. Pain made our desire clear.*

The Great Disappointment

When things don't disappoint us, we know that we don't care about them. When things disappointment us a little bit, we know that we care a little bit. But when we feel *great disappointment,* we know whatever caused it matters an awful lot.

Adventism was distilled by the Great Disappointment of October 22, 1844. How Adventists reacted to what didn't happen on that day clarifies the content of this Christian faith stream. Here's what some Adventists who experienced October 22 said about what it meant to them.

> *Henry Emmons:* "I waited all Tuesday and *dear Jesus* did not come. I waited all forenoon of Wednes-

* Miracle of miracles, and miracle of miracles again, we now have two children, born without the aid of modern fertility science.

day, and was well in body as I ever was, but after 12 o'clock I began to feel faint, and before dark I needed someone to help me up to my chamber, as my natural strength was leaving me fast, and I lay prostrate for two days without any pain—sick with disappointment."[1]

Washington Morse: "That day came and passed, and the darkness of another night closed in upon the world. But with that darkness came a pang of disappointment to the Advent believers that can find a parallel only in the sorrow of the disciples after the crucifixion of *their Lord*. The passing of time was a bitter disappointment. True believers had given up *all for Christ,* and had shared His presence as never before. *The love of Jesus filled every soul; and with inexpressible desire they prayed, 'Come, Lord Jesus, and come quickly;' but He did not come.*"[2]

Hiram Edson: "Our fondest hopes and expectations were blasted, and such a spirit of weeping came over us as I never experienced before. It seemed that *the loss of all earthly friends* could have been no comparison. We wept, and wept, till the day dawn."[3]

Seventeen-year-old Ellen White: "Those who *sincerely love Jesus* can appreciate the feelings of those who watched with the most *intense longing* for the coming of their Saviour."[4]

All religious movements have a beginning. They have a foundational, formational, inaugural, initial reason for existence.

- Judaism was born as an organized religion when Moses heard God's voice atop Mount Sinai.
- Islam sprang from the belief that Allah revealed insights to the Prophet Muhammad, who lived about fourteen hundred years ago. The Koran contains these revelations.
- Christianity was conceived in response to the life, death, and resurrection of Jesus of Nazareth. A group of men and women believed what He said about Himself and about them. They believed He rose from the dead, so they believed *Him*.

For two thousand years, all sorts of Christian sects, movements, denominations, organizations, and reorganizations have come to be.

- Because of theological and political differences, Christianity split into Eastern and Western churches in the A.D. 1054 Great Schism.
- The Church of England was founded in 1534, when,

due to a personal and political rift, King Henry VIII declared himself head of the church in place of the pope.

- The desire to reform the Roman Catholic Church eventually gave birth to Lutheranism and other Protestant traditions.
- Methodism was launched because of the piety of Charles and John Wesley.
- Convictions about liturgy (Was baptism for children or adults? Was *this* music or *that* music acceptable? Should the worship experience favor emotionalism or an emotion-free experience?) were behind the founding of some movements.
- Some groups were born out of a disagreement over a social issue such as the role of women or homosexuals in the church.
- Some began in opposition to, or support of, some doctrinal issue.
- Some began opposing or supporting violence or war.
- Some began because of the teaching of some particular theologian.
- Some were born out of deep-seated conflict, while others seemed to rise merely from the desire to do religion differently.
- Many began because a man or woman claimed to have had special or secret encounters with an angel or with God Himself.

Adventism wasn't born as a reform movement, though it soon adopted various reforms. Adventism wasn't born as a temperance movement, though it found something to say about healthful living. Adventism wasn't born as a theological movement, as a correction of already existing denominations, nor in response to some liturgical or lifestyle concern. And despite its prophet, Adventism didn't come into being because of unique, private prophetic revelations. Adventism was born because of a *wrong* calculation about the Second Coming . . . fueled by an intense, emotional, highly personal, fervent, and *ultimately right* desire to be with Jesus.

Adventism—*primal Adventism*—was about men and women who longed to be with Jesus.

The Desire of the Ages

The stream of Adventism is fed by the teardrops of the Great Disappointment. The cries of pain at its birth reveal intense affection and love for Jesus and an unsurpassed longing to be with Him. This is Adventism distilled. This is Adventism made most clear.

What makes Adventists unique? How would you answer this question?

I'd answer it by pointing to our unique beginning. Adventism isn't peculiar or special because of our Sabbath keeping, vegetarian cuisine, or remnant claims. Adventism's uniqueness is found at its historical root: Jesus.

Whatever else has been thrown into these Adventist waters over the past 170 years (much of it good, though perhaps some of it not so good), the river of this religion is all about loving Christ.

Adventism's nearly two-century-old hang-up is . . . Jesus.

I slid the back door open to let the dog out. Helium balloon in hand, Audrey, our four-year-old theologian, asked, "Daddy, if I let this go, would it go all the way up to Jesus?"

I paused to reflect on what answer I should give. (You have to be careful about these things.) "Yes," I said. "It would go all the way up to Jesus."

She pondered that lofty reality for a quiet moment or two. "Well, Daddy, when would He get it back to me?"

I had to think about that a little longer. "Soon," I said. "Soon."

Adventism *at its best* takes the balloons of life and somehow hears what they say about Jesus—the balloons of work and play, joy and sorrow, holiness, theology, doctrine, priorities, relationships, and even church. When we find Jesus in the middle of our lives, we are on the right track. When we worship and love Him, and when His love moves us to serve and love others, Adventism shines.

Jesus today. Jesus now.

Adventism *at its best* also looks up. It searches the skies with the very same hope that the Adventists of October 22, 1844, had. To be with Jesus. To enter His embrace and find a world without suffering and pain; sans tears and disappointment.

Adventism—again, *at its best*—has eyes that look up . . . not with fear-mongering predictions about the end of the world, not with wild speculations about when it will happen and how. Instead, with eyes that are filled with hope, humility, and love.

Jesus, later today—and if not today, then tomorrow.

The One

Is Jesus worth the tears and the desire? This enduring and endearing passion?

John 3:16 says, "God so loved the world, that he gave his only begotten Son" (KJV).

"Only begotten"? The Word is actually *monogenēs*. *Mono:* unique, one, one of a kind. Monochrome: one color. Monotone: one pitch. Monopoly: one who has it all.

The One.

The look. The sound. The One who has it all.

Genēs: genetics, human genes, *Homo sapiens,* DNA.

A One-of-a-kind human being.

There have been, and there are, lots of human beings—billions and billions over many generations. But God did something special in this one case. God poured God—all of God—into a human zygote. A human egg from one of Mary's ovaries, fertilized by the Spirit. And nine months later He was born: the Superhuman.

The beginning of Adventist anthropology—the search for who we are as human beings, our meaning, our purpose, our existence, our gene pool—is in the *monogenēs,* Jesus Christ. Not just any Jesus. Not just a word we use to fill in whatever secular scheme or religious regime we concoct. Jesus, the historical. Jesus, the real. The one-and-only Jesus. The Jesus of the Gospels. The One who holds certain values. Particular priorities. A very definite view of God, humanity, and the earth.

Jesus isn't a big deal. Jesus is *The Deal.*

First John 5:12 makes this bold claim: "He that hath the Son hath life; and he that hath not the Son of God hath not life" (KJV). So we can say, The denomination that hath the Son hath life; and the denomination that hath not the Son of God hath not life.

Adventism was born nearly two centuries ago in "the global West." But now in America, Europe, and Australia, Adventism finds itself (along with many other branches of Christianity) facing great challenges.

But the future of Adventism doesn't rest in master plans and master prayers. The future of Adventism doesn't find its hope in church structure, finances, new ways of articulating truth, creative approaches to theology, new or old worship, old-fashioned or new-fashioned ideas, or a longing for tomorrow or for yesterday. The future of Adventism is neither top down nor bottom up.

So what *is the future*? Here's my proposal: If Adventism is to have a bright, energetic, vibrant future . . . If Adventism is going to get a life and have a life . . . it must—*we* must—have the Son.

In 1842, during this era of Advent hope, fifteen-year-old Ellen White had a mystical experience. Her memoir points us to the heart of this movement. We end this chapter with Ellen White's *Green Cord Dream.*

> Soon after this I had another dream. I seemed to be sitting in abject despair, with my face in my hands, reflecting like this: If Jesus were upon earth, I would go to Him, throw myself at His feet, and tell Him all my sufferings. He would not turn away from me; He would have mercy upon me, and I would love and serve Him always.
>
> Just then the door opened, and a person of beautiful form and countenance entered. He looked upon me pitifully, and said: "Do you wish to see Jesus? He is here, and you can see Him if you desire it. Take everything you possess, and follow me."
>
> I heard this with unspeakable joy, and gladly gathered up all my little possessions, every treasured trinket, and followed my guide. He led me to a steep and apparently frail stairway. As I began to ascend the steps, he cautioned me to keep my eyes fixed upward, lest I should grow dizzy and fall. Many others who were climbing the steep ascent fell before gaining the top.
>
> Finally we reached the last step, and stood before a door. Here my guide directed me to leave all the things that I had brought with me. I cheerfully laid

them down. He then opened the door, and bade me enter. In a moment I stood before Jesus. There was no mistaking that beautiful countenance; that expression of benevolence and majesty could belong to no other. As His gaze rested upon me, I knew at once that He was acquainted with every circumstance of my life and all my inner thoughts and feelings.

I tried to shield myself from His gaze, feeling unable to endure His searching eyes; but He drew near with a smile, and laying His hand upon my head, said, "Fear not." The sound of His sweet voice thrilled my heart with a happiness it had never before experienced. I was too joyful to utter a word, but, overcome with emotion, sank prostrate at His feet. While I was lying helpless there, scenes of beauty and glory passed before me, and I seemed to have reached the safety and peace of heaven. At length my strength returned, and I arose. The loving eyes of Jesus were still upon me, and His smile filled my soul with gladness. His presence awoke in me a holy reverence and an inexpressible love.

My guide now opened the door, and we both passed out. He bade me take up again all the things I had left without. This done, he handed me a green cord coiled up closely. This he directed me to place next my heart, and when I wished to see Jesus, take it from my bosom, and stretch it to the utmost. He cautioned me not to let it remain coiled for any length of time, lest it should become knotted and difficult to straighten. I placed the cord near my heart, and joyfully descended the narrow stairs, praising the Lord, and telling all whom I met where they could find Jesus.[5]

---

1. George Knight, *A Search for Identity: The Development of Seventh-day Adventist Beliefs* (Hagerstown, Md.: Review and Herald® Publishing Association, 2000), 53; emphasis added.

2. George Knight, *A Brief History of Seventh-day Adventists,* 2nd ed. (Hagerstown, Md.: Review and Herald®, 2004), 25; emphasis added.

3. Ibid.; emphasis added.

4. Ellen G. White, *Life Sketches of Ellen White* (Mountain View, Calif.: Pacific Press® Publishing Association, 1915), 56; emphasis added.

5. Ibid., 34–36.

CHAPTER 2 HUMANITY

ADVENTISTS, IN THE BEGINNING, and at our best, put all of our eggs in one Basket: *Jesus Christ.*

In chapter 1, we saw that primal, original, foundational Adventism was all about a desire to be with Jesus. The founders of the church, including Ellen White, had a deep, emotional connection to Jesus. That connection was at the heart of the embryonic movement. Adventism, on its game, *always* keeps a focus on Jesus now, in this present life, while simultaneously looking upward in angst-free anticipation of the loving embrace of Jesus at His second coming. The future health and vitality of our Advent movement rests—*totally*—in "having the Son," through whom we have life, and in whom we enjoy life.

Adventism *aright* places all of its eggs in this one Basket. All of our salvation. All of our doctrines. All of our understanding of human origins, of earth history, of ethics, of sexuality, of money, of human relationships, of church practice, of death, and of the future. Jesus has absolute authority over absolutely everything.

This is an audacious statement.

A statement that has *consequences.*

- If we add three and two, a mathematics professor would say the consequence is five.
- If we put an *s* at the end of the word *cake,* an English teacher would say the result is more than one cake.
- If we put one million pounds on a bridge rated for half a million, an engineering instructor would say the ramification is a broken bridge.
- If I put two hundred pounds on a bench-press machine, a physical education expert would call an ambulance.

If *this,* then *that.* There are consequences. We can't throw Jesus language around without creating ramifications.

Historically, Adventism has wrapped itself in the New Testament book of Revelation, which contains some of the strongest claims of the supremacy of Jesus. The Bible's concluding book is decisive in its opinion of Jesus. Here are seven revelatory statements:

- "Jesus Christ, [is] the faithful witness, the firstborn from the dead, and the ruler over the kings of the earth" (Revelation 1:5, NKJV).

- "I am the Alpha and the Omega, the Beginning and the End, . . . who is and who was and who is to come, the Almighty"; "the First and the Last" (Revelation 1:8; 22:13, NKJV).
- "I am the Living One; I was dead, and now look, I am alive for ever and ever! And I hold the keys of death and Hades" (Revelation 1:18, NIV).
- "You are worthy, our Lord and God, to receive glory and honor and power, for you created all things, and by your will they were created and have their being" (Revelation 4:11, NIV).
- "In a loud voice they were saying: 'Worthy is the Lamb, who was slain, to receive power and wealth and wisdom and strength and honor and glory and praise!' " (Revelation 5:12, NIV).
- "They will wage war against the Lamb, but the Lamb will triumph over them because he is Lord of lords and King of kings" (Revelation 17:14, NIV).
- "I saw heaven standing open and there before me was a white horse, whose rider is called Faithful and True. With justice he judges and makes war. His eyes are like blazing fire, and on his head are many crowns. He has a name written on him that no one knows but he himself. He is dressed in a robe dipped in blood, and his name is the Word of God. The armies of heaven were following him, riding on white horses and dressed in fine linen, white and

> clean. Coming out of his mouth is a sharp sword with which to strike down the nations. He will rule them with an iron scepter. He treads the winepress of the fury of the wrath of God Almighty. On his robe and on his thigh he has this name written: King of kings and Lord of lords" (Revelation 19:11–16, NIV).

Saying with conviction that Jesus is the King of kings and Lord of lords has consequences—for Adventists as well as for other people. What are those consequences? That's what the rest of this book is about. What does it mean to live green-cord dreams? For Jesus to be One and All? What does an Adventism baptized by the Spirit of Christ look like?

The beginning

Let's begin here. Adventists view humanity in a particular way, and the view they have of others grows out of how they view themselves in relation to Jesus Christ.

The prototypical Adventist is the first-century gospel figure John the Baptist, who could also justifiably be named *John the Adventist*—after all, his job was to prophesy about the soon coming of the Messiah, Jesus Christ, the first time around. What can we learn from him and the way he viewed his relationship to Jesus? Notice what he said about Jesus and himself:

- "He who comes after me has surpassed me because he was before me" (John 1:15, NIV).
- "But one who is more powerful than I will come, the straps of whose sandals I am not worthy to untie" (Luke 3:16, NIV).
- "I baptize you with water, but he will baptize you with the Holy Spirit" (Mark 1:8, NIV).
- "He must become greater; I must become less" (John 3:30, NIV).
- "John tried to deter him, saying, 'I need to be baptized by you, and do you come to me?' " (Matthew 3:14, NIV).
- "The friend who attends the bridegroom waits and listens for him, and is full of joy when he hears the bridegroom's voice. That joy is mine, and it is now complete" (John 3:29, NIV).

John told his own disciples Peter and Andrew to follow Jesus. The goal of this Adventist leader was to direct Adventists toward Jesus. We're not supposed to be disciples of the Adventist, but disciples of Jesus Christ (John 1:35, 36).

John didn't spend a lot of time thinking, writing, and talking about what made him unique, special, and called. He wasn't concerned about his own identity. Even though he had a prophetic message, he wasn't concerned about his status as a prophet; he pointed people to Jesus. His diet was unusual: locusts and honey; but he didn't focus on what people should eat, but on Jesus. He dressed more simply than did his contemporaries, in clothing of camel's hair; however, he wasn't concerned with his appearance, he wanted people to see Jesus.

Over and over again, John the Adventist demoted himself and promoted Jesus. Ironically, it was in selflessly talking about Jesus that he discovered his own identity. The less he focused on himself, the more of himself he found.

Jesus said that of all the men born of women, none is greater in the kingdom of heaven than John the Baptist . . . yet he is the least of all (Matthew 11:11). Greatest *and* least? Another irony. John's *humility* makes him a great human being. The Adventist of Adventists doesn't obsess over the meaning of his Adventism. Instead, he persistently proclaims Christ.

My youngest brother was the first of my siblings to get married. It was to be a summer wedding, on a beach. That January I decided to start working out. Lifting weights. Running. Getting in shape for the big event. I faithfully invested time in the gym for weeks. One day, when I was in the weight room, I noticed that I was all alone. I walked up to the mirror that spanned the breadth of the gym wall, checked again to make sure I had the place to myself, and then raised my arms and flexed and admired my barely emerging biceps. A smile crept over my face as I assessed the "obvious" progress.

This magical moment, which was meant only for my

mirror image and me, was broken when a more distant image in the mirror came into focus. There *he* was. A man. A man who'd been working out not for weeks but for years. A man whose arms closely approximated the size of my legs. Big and buff; tanned and, I'm sure, tantalizing to the opposite sex. The image in the mirror had, first, a look of puzzlement and then of quiet amusement as he stared at me and at my image in the mirror. And then he said, "Keep posing there, boy."

I was horrified.

How silly we look when we tout our church, our religion, our denomination—when we *pose* with our holiness and flex our spiritual muscles to show just how righteous we are! When we look into the mirror and admire the body of our own faith tradition. Our insights. Our brain power. Our prophetic or theological prowess. When we brag about our biblical biceps and strut our spiritual stuff.

But when we look more deeply into the mirror, we see another, superior image.

Chapter 1 of Hebrews calls Him "the image of the invisible God." He is Jesus Christ. When we finally look at Him and see His beauty, His strength, His perfection, His power—we are red-faced. Then we must fall to our knees. We must confess the sin of worshiping ourselves rather than our Creator.

"Me monsters"

The American comedian Brian Regan has a routine I

love. It's all about people whom Regan calls "me monsters." These are people who feel the need to dominate every discussion. To talk about their adventures. Their problems. Their successes. Their travels. Themselves.

Regan goes on to imagine that he is one of the twelve men who have walked on the moon. How great it must be, he dreams, to sit back at a dinner party, listening to some conversation-dominating "me monster" go on and on about his working trips to Europe, his vacations at Aspen, the money he makes, the cars he drives, and on and on. And when he finally stops to catch a breath, the Apollo astronaut simply says, "I walked on the moon." Conversation over. An astronaut can shut the mouth of the self-absorbed "me monster" every time.

Jesus is the One who *hung* the moon. He's the Sun of Righteousness, the Bright and Morning Star. For Him the sky *isn't* the limit.

Critics would say that in Catholicism, the biggest rival to Jesus is the veneration of Mary or of a pope. Critics would say that in some Protestant churches, political leaders have replaced God. Critics would say that Mormon theology has relegated Christ to a lesser role than that of the Father God. Critics would say that some people worship the celebrity leaders of contemporary worship movements more than the One whom the songs are about.

Adventist Christians must beware of identifying with John the Adventist more than with the One whose advent we preach. We must beware of dwelling upon our own prophetic identity more than upon the identity of Jesus Christ.

The *greatest* threat to Adventism's future is not slippage in lifestyle, changes in liturgy, or a shrinking financial base. The supreme challenge is whether or not we will hold a collective belief in a very big Jesus Christ whose life argues for the existence and activity of a powerful and good God. The big issue is whether we worship a small Jesus or a large Jesus. A weak Christ or a strong Christ. Whether we will be self-absorbed or Savior-absorbed.

I believe Adventism will catch its stride and run like never before when Adventists focus on Jesus rather than themselves. John's advent purpose was successful because he talked little about what it meant to be an Adventist and much about the One who was to come and what His coming meant to the world. We'll find success in accomplishing our mission and fulfillment of our organization's purpose when we keep our eyes on Him.

Confessing Jesus as KING OF KINGS AND LORD OF LORDS has implications. It means that the duty of Adventists is not to honor the messenger—or the message—but the One whom the message is all about. And so we live a humble ecclesiology. We preach a humble church. This fact informs the way we relate to the whole of humanity. It prompts us toward a generous ecclesiology, toward a table open to fellowship with everyone. In other words, it prompts us toward the practice of open communion.

Think of it this way. A mayor draws a city together. The fact that all the citizens live under the authority of the mayor should cause them to want a rich local community spirit—for they're all under the same authority. That's their common bond. A governor draws together those who inhabit a state. The fact that they live in the same state gives them a connection and even a kind of camaraderie. This bond encompasses more people than does the city. A president or prime minister draws a nation together. The fact that the citizens live in the same nation, share connectivity, and are drawn toward mutual support and even teamwork should make them feel patriotic. This is an even larger bond.

Well, . . .

Jesus isn't a mayor.

He isn't a governor.

He isn't a president or prime minister.

He's the King of kings and Lord of lords!

He's the Ruler of the universe.

He's also the Parent of all.

If we take Jesus seriously, recognizing that He has jurisdiction and life-or-death power over every human being, then we should see one another as fellow citizens, subjects of the same kingdom. Switching metaphors: if all of us are children of God because He created all of us, then we are . . . *siblings*!

Only one body

If all Adventists are children of the same Father, how

should we act toward one another?

We might have our honest differences. We might challenge one another's beliefs and behaviors. But above all this, we will follow the example of our Father God, treating each other with the love and respect we see in strong, caring families.

If all Christians are children of the same Mother, how should we regard one another? Adventism has experienced more than one season of struggle over the question, "Are we Christian or cult?" Are we a separate body of Christ, or does Christ have—as Paul says in 1 Corinthians 1 and Ephesians 4—only one body?

Adventism has something particular and important to say to the whole of Christianity—a message unique to us. But we are brothers and sisters of all Christians around the world who proclaim Jesus as the Christ. We haven't been given the authority to delegitimize the sonship, daughtership, or siblingship of Christ-followers who differ from us in belief and behavior. Adventists can be true to their John the Baptist calling while sitting at the Thanksgiving table with Christian brothers and sisters.

If all people are, in fact, brothers and sisters, how should we look at one another? The Bible doesn't indicate that any human being who draws breath was made by a different creator. The God we worship is the Father of all. So as Christians and particularly as Adventist Christians engage the world, we do so viewing others not as the enemy but as beloved siblings whom we hope will come to know God, our Divine Father, in a more accurate and affectionate way.

I've had more fights with my brother David than with all the other people on planet Earth combined—ask my parents. David and I have argued, yelled, punched, pinched, and pounded. He'd dump a cup of cold water on me, and I'd start beating him with my fists. Then he'd yell to our grandmother, who lived across the street, "Grandma, Alex is trying to kill me!"

Which was true.

We still, as adults, have disagreements about sports, politics, and religion. But David would go to the ends of the earth for me, and I would do the same for him. David would defend me to the *nth* degree, and I would defend him. He loves me, and I love him.

We are debaters, arguers, disputants. But we are brothers *first.*

Why?

Do I need to explain the birds and the bees?

We are boys of the *same womb.* His egg and my egg were carried in the same basket.

And that means something.

Every Adventist, every Christian, every human being, is a child of the same Womb. We are all eggs of the same Basket. No one gives life but God, and no one who has life got it from anyone else but Jesus Christ.

And that means something.

Adventism aright views all of humanity as brothers and

sisters in need of their precious Creator—the FATHER OF ALL FATHERS, THE MOTHER OF ALL MOTHERS, THE KING OF ALL KINGS, AND THE LORD OF ALL LORDS.

Adventism, at its best, holds a humble and generous ecclesiology—a view of itself that gives all glory to Christ and all love to our human community.

Why?

Because we take Jesus seriously.

Chapter 3
Ears and Ink

Does God have a voice?

A friend of mine was praying with her young daughter a few weeks ago. Partway through her prayer, her daughter pleaded, "Wait, Mommy!"

"Wait?" my friend asked, puzzled.

"Yes. Be quiet, Mommy," she whispered. "Give God a chance to talk."

A long moment of silence ensued, eventually broken by the little girl's words. "Oh, never mind. He never really says anything."

We live in a world of words. The first act of a newborn baby is to take a deep breath and then to speak: *I don't like it out here! It's cold. It's bright. I'm hungry. Do something about it! I want to go back inside where it's warm and comfy.*

We're born wanting to make ourselves known, to communicate. We engage in a neonatal act of self-revelation. We *reveal* ourselves. What were the doctor, the nurse, and our parents looking for that would indicate our health, our life, our humanness? *Our first cry; our first communication!*

And we spend the rest of our lives talking and listening to other people talk. We tell stories. We give direction. We express opinions. We write. We type. We text. We Facebook. We join a World Wide Web of conversation—a human network of dialogue under construction since Creation. Human-to-human revelations about pregnancy, job loss and gain, new love found and lost, joy, sorrow, food, travel, sports, art, insights, depression, impressions, questions, and answers.

But like my friend's daughter, we long to hear another Voice. We need to hear from the One who made this masterpiece of a world—from the One who allows it to be such a mess. We need to know if there is a present and a future.

We need to hear from Someone above. We can't survive on the stories we tell one another. Weather forecasts, political speeches, and public service announcements aren't enough. We need more than gossip and prognostications. We need more than mere human voices. We need to hear the Word of God. We need the First Cause to speak.

Seventh-day Adventists, historically, have been known as a "people of the Book." The founding Adventists poured themselves into the Bible and poured the Bible into themselves. In its first days, the movement was marked by men and women who loved and respected Holy Scripture. We might say that the venue for the Advent vision was in thin pages bound by leather. The Adventist arena of activity was in the pages of the Bible. In the Sixty-Six.

There the pioneers found promises. Predictions. History. Future. Judgment. Truth. Authority. Explanation. And hope.

Adventism's sanctuary isn't a cathedral. Adventism's Holy Land, its Mecca, isn't found on a map. Adventism's mission statement isn't discovered on a plaque, in a work of systematic theology, or in an image, logo, or catch phrase.

Adventism's sanctuary is the Bible. Our *geography,* if you will, is the Bible. Our mission: to work and play in Scripture and then to work and play Scripture into life.

Adventism, at its best, loves the Word of God.

With all due respect to Adventism's association with passages like Daniel 8 and Revelation 14, I think Psalm 19:7–10 best captures the heart of our movement's ethos.

> The law of the Lord is perfect,
> refreshing the soul.
> The statutes of the Lord are trustworthy,
> making wise the simple.
> The precepts of the Lord are right,
> giving joy to the heart.
> The commands of the Lord are radiant,
> giving light to the eyes.
> The fear of the Lord is pure,
> enduring forever.

The decrees of the Lord are firm,
    and all of them are righteous.
They are more precious than gold,
    than much pure gold;
they are sweeter than honey,
    than honey from the honeycomb (NIV).

Adventists dig the Word, for God speaks and God cares. He is awake and alive and engaged. The Bible is God's sound wave, His music, His whisper, His shout, His story. The Bible is supersweet like honey. It breaks the bland human-to-human conversation, which can only take us so far.

This movement's preachers and teachers have given me three gifts—three pieces of advice that have taught me how best to engage the Bible. I've learned that Adventists who are on their game embrace these gifts, these treasures. When they remember and apply them, the Bible is transformational. But when they neglect them, it loses its beauty and bite.

Gift one: Don't obsess about the frying pan

The business leadership guru Tom Peters tells about a time when he was in his kitchen, washing a dirty frying pan. Hard work. Scrubbing out each grease stain takes a long time. Restoring the pan to its original pristine state is no quick and easy project—if, in fact, such perfection is even possible.

Peters finally concluded, *This is a waste of time! I'm going to spend so much time scrubbing this frying pan that I'll miss more important things.*[1] Like eating. Like eating with friends. Like cleaning cups, glasses, bowls, plates, forks, knives, and spoons. Like engaging in a whole host of other chores and responsibilities, opportunities, and adventures.

We can spend so much time in the demanding work of achieving frying-pan perfection that we miss what is truly best: life.

I learned this from Adventists: the pan of obsessive biblical analysis can divert our eyes and hearts from the panacea of the Spirit's vision for us. Hyperfocus on a given word or phrase can be destructive. The Bible can do wonderfully great work in our lives. It can cook up a rich spiritual meal that will leave us well nourished. But we have to eat it, to devour it, and we mustn't spend all our time trying to make it (and other people) perfectly clean.

The Bible is, after all, a dirty pan.

The book *Seventh-day Adventists Believe . . .* puts forth this good Adventist understanding: "Divine revelation was given by inspiration of God to 'holy men of God' who were 'moved by the Holy Spirit' (2 Peter 1:21). These revelations were embodied in human language with all its *limitations* and *imperfections,* yet they remained God's testimony. God inspired men—not words."[2]

God inspired thoughts, but He left it up to human beings to put them on parchment and papyrus. God prompted human beings to journal their experiences with Him, but He didn't get into the matter of nouns, verbs, and adjectives.

God wasn't the copy editor; He was *the Inspiration.* He could have dictated every word, but He didn't choose to do this—and we can be glad He didn't.

Why?

We can spend so much time arguing about a word, a phrase, or a particular meaning that we miss the grand sweep of Scripture. The larger point. We can spend so much time with a problematic phrase or a difficult passage—trying to scrub every grease stain from the frying pan—that we miss the meal.

The Bible has many major themes that are perfectly clear and that it articulates over and over again: God's love. Our need to love Him and to love one another. Grace. Morality. Sacrifice. Sexual fidelity. Care for the poor. Humility. Forgiveness. Faithfulness. Justice. Financial prudence—and more.

In my experience, Adventism's theological fistfights ("semantic skirmishes of sin"?) generally don't involve big, clear, obvious, well-attested themes. They involve problematic passages, obscure meanings, wrestling over words, metaphors, suggestions—matters that the Bible leaves opaque. Theological friction within the Adventist Church often seems to sprout in the soil of *lesser questions.*

Adventism at its best isn't obsessed with small arguments.

Adventism at its best isn't sidetracked by theological tangents. Adventism at its best is about *grand themes*—and there is no grander theme than Christ.

Again from *Seventh-day Adventists Believe . . .* :

> Jesus Christ is *the focus* of Scripture. The Old Testament sets forth the Son of God as the Messiah, the world's Redeemer; the New Testament reveals Him as Jesus Christ, the Saviour. Every book, either through symbol or reality, reveals some phase of His work and character. Jesus' death on the cross is the ultimate revelation of God's character. . . . The theme of God's love, particularly as seen in Christ's sacrificial death on Calvary—the grandest theme of the universe—is *the focus* of the Bible. All major Bible truths, therefore, should be studied from this perspective.[3]

Amid a fierce debate over Sabbath theology and practice, Jesus said, "You study the Scriptures diligently because you think that in them you have eternal life. These are *the very Scriptures that testify about me,* yet you refuse to come to me to have life" (John 5:39, 40, NIV; emphasis added).

The point of the Bible is not the Bible. The point is Jesus. Adventism aright doesn't remove every stain from scriptural pans. Instead, we eat the rich meal of Jesus Christ, stirred in the pan of God's written revelation, warmed by the Holy Spirit's fire. The Bible helps bring God's great banquet to us.

Gift two: Speak for yourself

I pastor on a college campus. Imagine a male student approaching me and saying, "Pastor, everyone knows that you are the doctor of love, the king of romance, the guru on how to woo college girls."

"True, my son," I would reply.

"Would you coach me, pastor? There's this girl, you see. Would you help me plan this all-important date?"

"Yes, my son. I will assist you."

"And pastor, will you come along on the date with us?"

"Yes, my son."

So, later that week I select the flowers, pick the restaurant, and rent the perfect car. I teach the young man surefire lines of verbal romance. We develop a system of signs so that during the date I can signal him about when to listen, when to speak, what to say, what to ask, and more.

The evening of the date arrives. We pick the girl up. I sit in the backseat, leaning forward between them, coaching every second of this experience, which I have planned.

Will this work? Will this approach engender love? Nope. In fact, it will certainly kill it. If I micromanage every aspect of this boy's relationship to this girl, *there will be no relationship.* I will have killed the relationship, destroyed the love.

I like to tease my friend Dave Thomas, who is dean of the School of Theology at Walla Walla University, where we both work. Ordinarily, he's a good-natured person with a wide and wonderful sense of humor. But to his dismay, I've taken to calling him the Chief Theological Officer on our campus. The Sheriff of Scripture. The Bible Boss.

My teasing makes him cringe. It bothers him because he's a good Adventist.

Let me say that again. *My teasing bothers him because he's a good Adventist.*

The Adventist pioneers were deeply concerned about doctrinal patrols. Religious liberty—the freedom to engage religion, church, and the Bible—wasn't merely an external concern; it was an internal value as well. Religious freedom was about life outside the church and life *inside* the church.

John Loughborough, a prominent Adventist preacher who was called to ministry by Ellen White, famously wrote, "The first step of apostasy is to get up a creed, telling us what we shall believe. The second is to make that creed a test of fellowship. The third is to try members by that creed. The fourth is to denounce as heretics those who do not believe that creed. And, fifth, to commence persecution against such."[4] Now, that's a strong statement! One quite representative of Adventists in the beginning—and of Adventists at their best in *every* era.

This is not to say that we should avoid serious dialogue about a correct reading of Scripture. We *should* refute theologies that aren't true—refute them in love and in humility, but firmly. Pastor Loughborough wasn't saying that *anything goes*. He was warning against an authoritarian perspective within the church that kills the desire to study the Bible. Obsessive monitoring of biblical study and interpretation *destroys* love for God's Word. Biblical babysitting robs men and women of the passion, curiosity, energy, and joy that studying these ancient documents should produce. An overbearing "chaperone" will snuff out the possibility of romance, of love, of marriage—of a lifelong commitment to God's Word.

The rabbis thought the *process* of biblical conversation was as important as the conclusions. The parables of Jesus didn't *end* the discussion, they *began* it. An Adventism that hushes up biblical dialogue kills the power of the text. But an Adventism that creates a safe and compelling environment for biblical dialogue and lets the text be wild, free, and transforming unleashes an awe-inspiring communion.

I love what Ellen White says about the continuing value of Bible study:

> There is no excuse for anyone in taking the position that there is no more truth to be revealed, and that all our expositions of Scripture are without an error. The fact that certain doctrines have been held as truth for many years by our people, is not a proof that our ideas are infallible. Age will not make error

> into truth, and truth can afford to be fair. No true doctrine will lose anything by close investigation.[5]

> *As real spiritual life declines,* it has ever been the tendency to cease to advance in the knowledge of the truth. Men rest satisfied with the light already received from God's Word, and discourage any further investigation of the Scriptures. They become conservative, and seek to *avoid discussion.*[6]

Spirituality *declines* as theological conversation is muted. Spirituality has the potential to *grow* where exploration is permitted, encouraged, and protected.

Gift three: Learn from the musician

Finally, a word about Ellen White, a human being who models love for the Bible. She was a "person of the Book."

Some Adventists *deify* Ellen White. Others *demonize* her. Some want to build a shrine in her honor, and others want to burn her books. I have grown to appreciate this woman as neither god nor godless, but good. She was neither deity nor demon, but a delight. In fact, I have found her to be inspirational.

Adventist historian George Knight quotes Ellen White's own statements about her function and purpose:

> Unlike some who claim to be modern prophets and whose followers treat their writings as kind of a

> third testament, Ellen White explained that her function was "to exalt" the Word of God "and attract minds to it, that the beautiful simplicity of truth may impress all" (5T, 665).
>
> She saw her purpose as bringing people "back to the Word that they have neglected to follow" (Ibid., 663).
>
> "The written testimonies," she asserted, "are not to give new light, but to impress vividly upon the heart the truths of inspiration already revealed" in the Bible (Ibid., 665).[7]

Maybe we can think about Ellen White and her writings this way: God is the Inspiration behind a piece of music—say Beethoven's Ninth Symphony. (My favorite.) So, too, God is the Inspiration behind all human works that reveal Him, especially the canon of Scripture.

Like Beethoven, the Bible writers were composers. They took the spiritual truths with which God inspired them and put them down on paper. Through poems, histories, prayers, stories, parables, prophecies, arguments, songs, and metaphors, they brought to life the music that God put in their souls.

Ellen White was a musician. She was the trumpeter, the violinist, the drummer. She did what great musicians always do: they *play* the Great Music. She took Beethoven's "Ninth" (the Bible) and brought this great work to life. Through her sermons, her books, her example, she made the type on the page *sing*. She loved Scripture's symphonies, and she played them with excellence—full of rhythm, melody, and mood.

And then she becomes prophetic. She becomes evangelistic, which is the natural bent of great musicians. She extends an invitation to us. She doesn't invite us to sit back in a pew and listen to her music. Instead, she challenges us to pick up an instrument ourselves! The point is that we're not to listen passively as she plays the music of the Bible; we're to be inspired by her love of the Written Word and join the orchestra! *Reading Ellen White shouldn't motivate us to read Ellen White, but to read and relish the Bible.*

Listen to the prophet:

> We should not take the testimony of any man as to what the Scriptures teach, *but should study the words of God for ourselves.* If we allow others to do our thinking, we shall have crippled energies and contracted abilities. The noble powers of the mind may be so dwarfed by lack of exercise on themes worthy of their concentration as to lose their ability to grasp the deep meaning of the Word of God. The mind will enlarge if it is employed in tracing out the relation of the subjects of the Bible, comparing

> scripture with scripture and spiritual things with spiritual.
>
> There is nothing more calculated to strengthen the intellect than the study of the Scriptures. No other book is so potent to elevate the thoughts, to give vigor to the faculties, as the broad, ennobling truths of the Bible. If God's word were studied as it should be, men would have a breadth of mind, a nobility of character, and a stability of purpose rarely seen in these times. . . .
>
> The words of inspiration, pondered in the heart, will be as streams flowing from the fountain of life.[8]

Adventists at their best are people of the Book—people who avoid scraping pans so they can enjoy the biblical feast; people who believe everyone should have the freedom to explore the Bible freely; people who themselves play the biblical music—melodic vibrations that sing of Jesus!

---

1. Tom Peters, *The Little Big Things: 163 Ways to Pursue Excellence* (New York: HarperStudio, 2010), 198.
2. *Seventh-day Adventists Believe . . .* (Washington, D.C.: Ministerial Association of the General Conference of Seventh-day Adventists, 1988), 14; emphasis added.
3. Ibid., 13; emphasis added.
4. George Knight, *A Search for Identity*, 22.
5. Ellen G. White, *Counsels to Writers and Editors* (Nashville: Southern Publishing Association, 1946), 35

6. Ibid., 39; emphasis added.

7. George Knight, *Reading Ellen White: How to Understand and Apply Her Writings* (Hagerstown, Md.: Review and Herald®, 1997), 16, 17; quoting Ellen G. White, *Testimonies for the Church* (Mountain View, Calif.: Pacific Press®, 1948), 5:663, 665.

8. Ellen G. White, *Steps to Christ* (Washington, D.C.: Review and Herald®, 1956), 89–91.

CHAPTER 4
COMPASSION

On Friday afternoon, August 14, 1909, at about 5 p.m., Sheriff Charles Werner of Springfield, Illinois, made a bold decision. He was holding two black men in his jail: Joe James and George Richardson. The first was accused of raping a woman, and the second had been arrested on suspicion of murder. An angry mob of about four thousand white people had set up camp outside the jailhouse. Their intent: to take justice into their own hands. Immediately.

Sheriff Werner concluded that the safety of his jail, the lives of his prisoners, and his own life were all in danger, so he decided to act. He called the fire department and requested that sirens-blaring, lights-flashing fire engines speed past the police station. It worked! It provided the distraction he needed. While the crowd was fixated on the fire engines, he sneaked the two men out, shuttling them on to a nearby town and then to the state penitentiary, where they were out of the reach of the mob and were assured of their day in court.

After the sheriff had gotten the accused out of harm's way, he told the mob that the men they wanted to harm were no longer there, and he invited a small search party made up of the mob's leaders to inspect the jailhouse for themselves. They confirmed that the two inmates had vanished. But rather than settling down when they discovered that the two men had slipped out, the mob grew even angrier and looked for outlets for their pent-up, racially charged rage. The violence began at about eight-thirty that evening. The target was Springfield's black community.

Neighborhoods and businesses were torched, and when firefighters arrived, their water hoses were cut. Fists struck bodies, bullets pierced flesh, and knives slashed throats of men, women, and children alike. Two men were lynched: Scott Burton, a barber, and eighty-four-year-old William Donegan, a cobbler.

The hate-driven bloodbath resulted in the deaths of seven people—one of them a tiny baby. Thousands of blacks were driven from the city never to return, and those who remained were marginalized—harassed, threatened, fired from jobs. And though 150 people who were suspected of inciting the violence were arrested, only one was found guilty.

The items below tell a sad story.

- From 1890 through 1909* nearly two thousand blacks were lynched in the United States. Forty years after the close of the Civil War, conditions for black Americans had gotten worse, not better.
- Voting rights had been taken away by unchecked intimidation and a series of legislative and judicial actions requiring would-be voters to pass literacy tests—almost impossible for blacks since they were excluded from quality public education.
- Life expectancy was forty-seven years for whites and just thirty-three years for blacks, a fourteen-year difference.
- Twenty thousand black babies died every year (one of every nine born).
- The best healthcare was reserved for whites.
- All well-paying jobs and sometimes all jobs period went to whites.
- Interracial marriage was illegal in many places.

Blacks were not treated merely as second-class citizens; they were treated as noncitizens—driven from social, political, economic, and communal life. In a nation full of Christians, human beings who were created in the image of God and for whom Christ died were treated like animals—and

* The NAACP—the National Association for the Advancement of Colored People—was founded in 1909, a year that shows up throughout this chapter.

sometimes worse than animals.

On her way East

In this world lived an elderly woman, who, at eighty-one years of age and in failing health, determined to make what would be her final trip from her Northern California home to the eastern United States, where she would make her final appearance at a General Conference session and deliver her final sermon to the leadership of the growing Christian movement called Adventism.

On April 5, 1909, Ellen White, the religious reformer, compassionate prophet, social revolutionary, and most of all, fervent lover of Jesus Christ, left her St. Helena home. She made four stops in Southern California before taking the Omaha Railroad across the Rockies to Union College, where she preached to the community of College View, Nebraska.[1]

From there, she headed, on the twentieth of April, to Nashville, Tennessee, where, in addition to meeting with the white congregations, she made an intentional and courageous decision to stop at Rock City Sanitarium and other church institutions designed for ministry to black people. She delivered a sermon to a black congregation in their house of worship on Winter Street in Nashville, saying,

> I recall how especially one of your race was recognized by God in the time of the apostles, the record

> of which we find in the book of Acts. The Ethiopian mentioned there was a man of influence, and was doing great work when he heard the message of the gospel. . . . I am glad that the message of Christ's second advent has reached so many of the colored people. I want to say to you, the Lord is no respecter of persons. He makes no difference . . . because of the color of your skin. He understands all your circumstances. We have one Saviour for all mankind.[2]

Later she challenged those at the school for whites in Madison, near Nashville, to pay attention to every field of ministry and mission, and she spoke specifically of their mandate as Christians to minister to those in the black community.

From Nashville, she traveled to Huntsville, Alabama, the home of what is now Oakwood University. The vocational and educational mission to blacks that was being conducted there was about to graduate its very first class. This stop gave substance to the daring words she had spoken at the 1891 General Conference, when, though under great fire for her progressive stance, she boldly proclaimed, "I do not mean to live a coward or die a coward The black man's name is written in the book of life beside the white man's. . . . Birth, station, nationality, or color cannot elevate or degrade men." Further, those who "slight a brother because of his color are slighting Christ."[3]

From Huntsville, she proceeded to Asheville, North Carolina, again visiting both the white and the black congregations. On May 1, she preached from a pulpit that still stands in the Foster Memorial Seventh-day Adventist Church, in South Asheville. Her sermon that day is not on record, but on Sunday morning, May 2, she worshiped with and preached to the black congregation, using John 15 as her text. In that passage, Jesus calls all Christians to minister as He ministered, strengthened by being connected to Him as branches are to a vine. This theme would ignite her presentations at the General Conference session soon to be held in Washington, D.C.*

She mentioned this Asheville visit in a May 11, 1909, letter: "On Sunday morning, I spoke to our colored brethren and sisters in their little church. We found a nice company assembled there, all dressed modestly. Tears were in the eyes of many as they expressed their great pleasure that I was able to meet with them. . . . I am very glad that I had opportunity to speak to this congregation in their house of worship."[4]

From Asheville, Ellen White traveled to the General Conference session, where she preached eleven times. Her theme was mission. Creative mission. Bold mission. All-inclusive mission. Generous mission. Sacrificial mission.

---

* Imagine the courage Ellen White revealed as she "pressed the flesh" on the church steps with black men and women in this Southern city!

Love-bathed mission to a hurting and broken world. Her keynote address, given on Sabbath, May 15, 1909, is a powerful prophetic exhortation. We will conclude our 1909 story with excerpts from that address—and then explore what her words mean regarding the purpose and possibilities that lie before Adventism more than one hundred years later.

> On my journey to Washington I had some experience in going not only to the highways, but also to the hedges. . . .
>
> On this journey to Washington I did not expect to speak in many places, but when I got within reach of the people I could not help doing all I could. My soul was so drawn out with earnest hope, with confidence that they would receive the message, that I spoke the word to the white people and to the colored people whenever opportunity was given me. . . .
>
> I thank God that I did not neglect the colored people. . . .
>
> God has given Christ as a pattern of what our lives should be. Do you see him walking in the streets, and looking upon and pitying the sick? His heart is drawn out in compassion for them. He weeps for the afflicted and the suffering. He draws them close to His heart of love, and heals them. . . .
>
> There is something for each of us to do. It is no

> use to talk of being Christians if we leave unhelped those who are perishing all around us. . . .
>
> As soon as Christ becomes an abiding presence in the heart, we shall not be able to see souls perishing. . . . We will make any sacrifice that we may reach them; and there are none of us so poverty-stricken but we can make sacrifices for Christ daily. . . .
>
> What the Lord wants now is men and women who have the missionary spirit, who understand why Christ gave His life, why He laid off His royal robe and kingly crown, and came to the world as a little child, to be brought up in poverty. . . .
>
> You may feel that you make sacrifices; but if you go where I have been, in the highways and hedges, your compassion will be stirred by what you see. May God help us, that we may work to the point. We need to pray, and to pray in faith. We need to carry forward the work that God have given us to do. Our children are to be saved; our neighbors are to be labored for; and we are to act as if eternal life meant something to us.[5]

Seventh-day Adventism, at its best, is deeply humanitarian. *Seventh-day Adventism,* aright, is humane. As we shall see, compassion is embedded in our name, *Seventh-day Adventists.* And because it's there, compassion should permeate our denominational culture.

First: *Seventh-day* Adventism

A few years ago, I, along with several other men from the Collegedale, Tennessee, Seventh-day Adventist congregation, enjoyed a rewarding experience involving ministry. We took turns leaving our homes to spend a night at St. Matthew's Homeless Shelter in downtown Chattanooga. It was our job to "chaperone" the facility from 6 P.M. to 6 A.M.

I met a man named Greg at the homeless shelter. He had just been released from an Alabama prison and was in the process of getting back on his feet. I liked Greg. He was interesting to talk to and always kind and helpful. But he never smiled. He brought it up himself. "Forgive me if I don't smile a lot," he said. "You see, I'm missing a tooth from a jailhouse fight." Then, using his fingers, he pulled his lips back, revealing not only the empty place where a tooth should have been, but also that the rest of his teeth were tobacco stained and obviously hygiene deprived.

Later that night as I lay on an old sofa in the homeless shelter, I felt the Holy Spirit's nudge: *Alex, you need to do something about Greg's smile.* I told this story to the Sabbath School class I attended and also to a skilled and compassionate dentist in the congregation. The generosity of both the members of the class and of the dentist enabled us to make Greg an offer that he didn't pass up. I played the role of chauffeur, making several trips from downtown Chattanooga to the dentist's office in Collegedale. Weeks later, Greg's many dental problems were resolved. He even made this commitment: "I don't want to mess up my new look, so I'm not using tobacco anymore."

I'll never forget the last trip we made from the dental clinic back to the homeless shelter where Greg was staying. He had pulled the passenger-side visor of my Honda Civic down so he could look into the diminutive mirror. He pulled his lips back again, baring his teeth. Then, with tears rolling down his cheeks, he said, "Look, Alex! I've got my smile back."

There's a relationship between Sabbath School and compassion. There's a relationship between Sabbatarianism and humanitarianism. Christian Sabbath keeping means following the example of the *Lord of the Sabbath,* Jesus Christ.

Did you know that the four Gospels tell of seven miracles of healing that Jesus performed on the Sabbath?

- The man with a withered hand (Matthew 12:9–13).
- The demon-possessed man (Mark 1:21–26).
- Peter's mother-in-law (Luke 4:38, 39).
- The bent-over woman (Luke 13:10–16).
- The man with dropsy (Luke 14:1–5).
- The crippled man at the pool of Bethesda (John 5:5–9).
- The man born blind (John 9:1–14).

I think it is fascinating that every case involves a chronic condition; we're not talking about sudden, unavoidable, immediate needs here. Sabbath keeping is about *routine* healing, compassion, and wholeness—not just dealing with emergencies. This must be why Jesus says the Sabbath was made for man—for human beings. Its purpose is humanitarian. Its purpose is humane. Sabbatarians who *are not* humane are not Sabbath keepers in the manner of Jesus.

Sabbath is for worship, yet Jesus doesn't emphasize this aspect of the day. Sabbath is for rest, yet Jesus doesn't emphasize rest either. Again and again, Jesus connects Sabbath and healing, Sabbath and compassion. For Jesus, being a Sabbath keeper means living as a keeper of people—especially those in need.

Jesus defines His ministry with a "signature" inaugural passage: Isaiah 61:1, 2 (which Luke quotes in his Gospel—chapter 4:18, 19). Jesus could use any one of many other Old Testament texts to introduce the meaning of His ministry—but He doesn't. He chooses this one:

> "The Spirit of the Lord is on me,
> because he has anointed me
> to proclaim good news to the poor.
> He has sent me to proclaim freedom for the prisoners
> and recovery of sight for the blind,
> to set the oppressed free,
> to proclaim the year of the Lord's favor" (NIV).

Jesus refers to "the year of the Lord's favor"—the jubilee.

He has in mind the sabbatical system of Leviticus—a system that was rich with compassion: compassion for the earth, compassion for the slave, compassion for the widow, the orphan, the man in debt. The most prominent component of Jesus' ministry is compassion.

There is yet another fascinating connection between Sabbath and compassion. Adventists have held that the Sabbath will be a critical issue in the final days of earth's history. We've already seen that Jesus binds the Sabbath and acts of compassion together in His teaching, in His miracles, and in the description of His mission that He drew from the Old Testament. Then there's Matthew 25. In this chapter, Jesus paints an end-time scene. Judgment. Sheep. Goats. Saved. Lost. The world divided in two.

And what's the issue? The end-of-time issue?

Did you feed Me when I was hungry?
Did you quench My thirst when I had no water?
Did you clothe Me when I was cold?
Did you include Me when I was lonely?
Did you visit Me when I was in prison?
Did you care for Me when I was sick?

In other words, the Judge who presides over the final judgment asks, Were you compassionate?

Adventist Sabbatarians ought to both speak up and act to

make potable water available to the two billion people in this world who can't get it now. We ought to expend a lot of energy confronting poverty, abuse, hatred, violence, and sexual crime around the world. We must work to end institutionalized racial segregation outside the church and within it. We must fight the good fight of making certain that both outside and inside the church, women are treated with the same dignity and are given the same opportunities as are men.

Jesus made the Sabbath. He knows what purpose it's meant to fill. And in His miracles, in His messianic commission, and in His portrayal of the judgment, we see ties between the Sabbath and compassion. Seventh-day living promotes seven-day-a-week humanitarianism.

Second: Seventh-day *Adventism*

Adventism understands its unique calling to be announcing the re-making of the earth. Jesus is coming again soon to make the world right again, and so we preach heaven.

Consider this.

What if all the Adventists in the world had to duct tape their mouths closed . . . and then do their best to describe heaven to earthlings?

Could they do it?

The author Shane Claiborne tells about a trip he took to India. His story goes something like this. He finds himself amid some of the poorest children in the world. They swarm around him, looking for some handout—for anything. Claiborne reaches into his pocket and discovers he has one piece of gum. He gives it to a little girl, and, to his astonishment, she rips the stick into little pieces so all the children can chew a piece of the gum.

Later, Claiborne buys an ice-cream cone for a little boy—and watches in amazement as the boy takes a lick and then passes the cone from child to child so that every child can have a taste.[6]

Preaching heaven without words. *This is what heaven will be like. Want to come?*

Last week I attended some pastoral meetings in Southern California. I brought my family along, and when the meetings were over, we went to Disneyland. When you enter that place, you enter *a totally different world.* In fact, there's a sign bearing a quotation from Walt Disney posted near the entrance: "Here you leave today and enter the world of yesterday, tomorrow, and fantasy."

A different world.

We rode roller coasters, met princesses, and had our pictures taken with oversized rodents. I felt like a good American and a good dad. (And a poor dad!) The highlight for me came late in our day—a ride I had been on years earlier as a child. We got into a little white boat that floated on clear, blue water. Slowly, gently, quietly, the current pushed us along. Then we heard the music. At first it was faint, but as we proceeded, it grew louder. And then, suddenly, there were images of children from every continent: red and yellow, black and white. Playing, dancing, singing. They were singing the same song over and over and over again. A song that proclaims that we live in a world of both laughter and tears, a world of both hopes and fears. A song that reminds us that "though mountains divide and the oceans are wide, it's a small world after all."

I found my soul filling with emotion. The children of Egypt and Ecuador. The children of Norway and North Korea. The children of South Africa and North America. At peace. Undivided. Neither Jew nor Greek; slave nor free; male nor female; black nor white.

Lion and lamb together.

One heaven.

I didn't want the ride to end. It seemed to be a hint of . . .

. . . the world of yesterday, in Eden.

. . . the world of tomorrow, in a new earth.

. . . a world of fantasy, of imagination, of hope.

The blessed hope, as Paul calls it in Titus 2:13: "We wait for the blessed hope—the appearing of the glory of our great God and Savior, Jesus Christ" (NIV).

The Appearing. The Second Appearing.

The Advent. When all will be right with the world. When humanity will be humane.

The Lord of the Sabbath calls us to compassion. The Lord of the Second Advent calls us to compassion.

May Seventh-day Adventists, Jesus-enriched, be *Seventh-day*

Adventists—and therefore be a people richly compassionate, richly humanitarian.

---

1. See Arthur L. White, *Ellen G. White: The Later Elmshaven Years* (Hagerstown, Md.: Review and Herald®, 1982). This work provides an excellent account of Ellen White's journey.

2. Manuscript 17, 1909. This document is accessible online at http://www.whiteestate.org/books/mol/Chapt19.html.

3. Ibid.

4. Letter 86, 1909, written May 11, 1909. The Web site www.whiteestate.org contains this and other documentation on her 1909 travels.

5. Excerpts from sermon accessed at http://www.adventistarchives.org/doc_info.asp?DocID=1952.

6. Shane Claiborne, *The Irresistible Revolution: Living as an Ordinary Radical* (Grand Rapids, Mich.: Zondervan, 2006), 165, 166.

Chapter 5
Humility

Adventists, at our best, are humble.

Adventism on its game advocates a lifestyle of humility.

Of course, we're at our best when we're under the influence of Christ, who is our first, primal, original, foundational love. Then we want a humble church, a humble community, a humble authority, humble politics, a humble leadership, a humble kingdom. Humility is part of Adventist discipleship—the way Adventists live their lives.

This was evident from the beginning—and made most clear by the movement's critique of its homeland: America. That's right; Adventism's birth certificate reads "United States of America." Even though less than 5 percent of Adventists live in America now, the relationship between America and Adventism is indelible. We can't escape it: Adventism is an American religion. But it's also, in many important ways, an anti-American religion. Pioneer Adventists, in fact, explained the church's mission, its theology, by *contrasting* it to the America of their day.

In their book *Seeking a Sanctuary: Seventh-day Adventism and the American Dream,* Keith Lockhart and Malcolm Bull argue that Adventism is just this intentional, alternative vision of life. They observe the following:

> If the American dream can be defined, it would include the following elements:
>
> (1) the belief that the American Revolution created a state uniquely blessed by God in which human beings have unprecedented opportunities for self-realization and material gain;
>
> (2) the conviction that the American nation, through both example and leadership, offers hope for the rest of the world; and
>
> (3) the assumption that it is through individual, rather than collective, effort that progress of humanity will be achieved.
>
> In their formative years, the Seventh-day Adventists rejected the essentials of the American myth. They did not accept that the republican experiment would lead to the betterment of humanity or that it would be a lasting success. They consigned America to eventual destruction, and in the place of the nation, they daringly submitted themselves as the true vehicle for the redemption of the world.

> America had offered sanctuary to generations of immigrants from Europe; Adventists sought to provide a sanctuary from America.[1]

Indeed, Adventists have written about, talked about, and prophesied about America extensively throughout their history. This is particularly true in Adventism's interpretation of the book of Revelation. Adventist theologians have understood the violent, arrogant, bloodthirsty, profane dragon of Revelation 12 as representing Satan himself, and they have understood the first beast of Revelation 13 to represent the iron-fisted, oppressive, destructive Rome—both civil and religious. Revelation 14, 16, 17, and 18 picture a power named *Babylon*. Adventists have considered Babylon to be not only the hellish empire that took Daniel captive in the sixth century B.C. but also as representative of all totalitarian regimes throughout history that crush human rights, and in particular, religious liberties.

And Adventists have identified the *second beast* of Revelation 13, which functions right in the middle of all of this, as representing the United States of America. We recognize America's goodness, but also America's evil.

Revelation 13:11 speaks of this mixed record. John wrote, "I saw a second beast, coming out of the earth. It had two horns like a lamb, but it spoke like a dragon" (NIV).

America is both lamb and dragon! This country, so said

early Adventists, is both tender and tyrannical; both helpful and hellish!

And Adventists have maintained that they offer a different power, one that stands in opposition to the American dream, the Roman dream, the Babylonian dream, and the dragon's dream. Adventism, in fact, speaks against all the human kingdoms of this world. We say No to the values that earthly kingdoms hold, and we support a different kind of kingdom—that of Jesus Christ.

What do earth's powers value? Three *G*s: guns, gold, and glory.

Guns

First, guns. Violence. Power. Coercion. Control. Adventists have held, historically, a "conscientious objection" to war, to bearing arms, to violence in all of its many forms.

This view stands in dramatic opposition to the culture we live in now, in the twenty-first century. Note the titles of some of the video games that were most popular in the year 2010:

BioShock 2
Tom Clancy's Splinter Cell: Conviction
Assassin's Creed II
Red Dead Redemption
Diablo 3
Battlefield: Bad Company 2
Dead Rising 2

Mass Effect 2
APB: All Points Bulletin
Aliens vs. Predator

Here's the description of a popular new game called *Bulletstorm:*

> Travel from scorched deserts to tropical forests and an adult playground resort on a beautifully realized paradise defiled, delivered by the power of the Unreal Engine. Combine outrageous gunplay with *Bulletstorm*'s unique kick, slide, and leash mechanics as you kill with skill, racking up points along the way.
>
> *Bulletstorm*'s upgrade system truly is a circle of awesome that rewards players who kill in the most creative ways. From your trusty Peace Maker Carbine to the explosive Flail Gun, *Bulletstorm* delivers an arsenal of the most inventive, death-dealing weapons ever seen that truly put the fun back into the First Person Shooter.[2]

Modern American entertainment is drenched in violence. The combination of the brutal mixed martial arts and cage fighting is attracting more fans than ever before. Classic American superheroes like Batman and Superman don't redeem the bad guys—they use violence to stop them. Movies rarely—if ever—tell stories in which those who are evil become good. Instead, they generally picture the good people, the heroes, violently destroying the evildoers. By the stories they tell, if not directly, they say that violence is the answer.

And domestic violence pervades our homes, and violent discourse marks our political and even our religious discussions. The United States has a violent history and a violent present. Our government spends more on weapons than do the next twenty countries combined.[3]

The theologian Walter Wink, in his book *Engaging the Powers,* writes,

> Violence is the ethos of our times. It is the spirituality of the modern world. It has been accorded the status of a religion, demanding from its devotees an absolute obedience to death. Its followers are not aware, however, that the devotion they pay to violence is a form of religious piety. . . . The roots of this devotion to violence are deep, and we will be well rewarded if we trace them to their source. When we do, we will discover that the religion of Babylon—one of the world's oldest continuously surviving religions—is thriving as never before in every sector of contemporary American life, even in our synagogues and churches. It, and not Christianity, is the real religion of America. . . . No other religious system has ever remotely rivaled the myth of redemptive

> violence in its ability to catechize its young so totally. From the earliest age children are awash in depictions of violence as the ultimate solution for human conflicts.[4]

And Adventism was born in this violent context.

We can appreciate America for its many fine qualities while also acknowledging its history as the only nation to drop atomic bombs and the nation that has built the strongest military in the world. We can love much about America, for there is much to love, while recognizing in a sober-minded way that this continent was taken by force—a conquest that included the mass slaughter of Native Americans. We can be appropriately patriotic and still admit the historic and present-day violence of our culture. We can respect and love our nation while at the same time rejecting those of its values that are demonic.

As a boy raised Adventist, I was taught that soldiers are to be honored. The man in uniform is to be given great respect. However, I was also taught that picking up a gun was something to be taken very seriously. Conscientious objection—saying No to bearing arms—was an important part of Adventist Christianity's ethos.

As a boy, I was taught caution in the matters of abortion and capital punishment. While Adventists were careful not to take hard-and-fast political viewpoints, a high regard for life was always assumed. Adventism was respectful of life, and humble and cautious about ending it. As a boy, I was taught that Adventism was about hospitals and healing, and that it was radically opposed to killing and destruction. While we didn't take the strict pacifistic approach of some religious groups, we were taught that careful consideration and a humble willingness to listen to the opponent, the enemy, were crucial matters, as were decisions about what and who we were allowed to kill.

Babylon told the world to bow down to the gold statue or else be thrown into the flames. Adventism said the threat of flames, of guns, of bombs, of torture, of violence—even in, especially in, the service of making the world right—is, in fact, wrong.

Adventism, I learned, loses one of its great gifts when it embraces violence, when it loses the call of its conscience to peace. It loses humility.

Gold

What is the worst job you've ever had?

Growing up, I repaired toilets.

Not my worst job.

I picked up garbage and cleaned trash containers.

Not my worst job.

I pulled weeds in the hot sun on a strawberry farm.

Not my worst job.

I sold dried fruit door to door. *That* was my worst job. Convincing people that they wanted to buy wrinkled apricots, parched apple slices, and has-been plums, grapes, and peaches. That was awful.

My parents made me do it. Hard work—it's good for you, they said. Learn to make money, and then save some of that money. Tithe some of that money. Give some to the poor. Be careful with money. Live simply. Money is dangerous. In fact, the love of it is the foundation of all evil.

The early Adventists warned against the purchase of bicycles and bracelets. It was a matter of frugality. These items were not cheap, and Adventists were to be careful about spending their money on expensive toys and jewels. They were to know better than to pour money into things that merely make a show—or that can show a person up as a fool. Reject debt. Live simply, within your means. Be cautious with cash and coin. And do all of this so that you can live at peace and invest generously in helping people—so you can participate in the passions of Jesus by doing the work of God in this world.

America is now broke, and Americans are drowning in debt. Saving is no longer practiced nor thought possible. Our fellow citizens are addicted to toys and trips. They no longer save. They pay off only when they're forced to.

And Adventists? Are individual Adventist men and women living a different value? Is the church? Are we spending less? Are we saving more? Are we giving more? Are we eliminating waste? Are we working at living more simply in our homes and in our church? Are we rejecting the trap of collecting stuff and thus freeing ourselves to live more freely and to give more generously to the great cause of freedom in Christ? Are we, as a denomination, being faithful stewards of the money God has placed in our hands to be used for His purposes?

My grandmother and grandfather, who worked at the world headquarters of the denomination, once told me they tried to combine personal travel and travel for the church. Why? So they could take the expense themselves and not have to bill the church.

Now that's countercultural.

They lived their lives simply: artfully, beautifully, generously—but simply. As church leaders, they were ruthless about keeping expenses down so people around the world could be touched with the word and the hug of the gospel. They *had* to get the money to the front lines.

Babylon had a gold statue. King Nebuchadnezzar said, Bow down to the gold. It's the one who has the gold who is worthy of worship.

People who believe that, live to get the gold, to show off the gold, to wear the gold, to drive the gold, to play with the gold. Life is all about the gold.

The first people who heard John's description of the heavenly city that God will bring to earth must have been tempted to shout with glee. The gold is there.

But the gold *won't* be in a statue. It will be in the streets.*

* See Revelation 21.

In God's kingdom, gold isn't worshiped; it's walked on!

Wow!

Gold won't belong to the few alone, but to all. The gold rush will be over. Gold won't be precious; people will be precious. But gold will be more beautiful than ever because it won't be hoarded, misused, worshiped.

Glory

Finally, glory.

Glory in our world is reserved for those in power. For those who are famous. For those who control the bombs, who control the airwaves, who control the markets, who control the corporations, and who control the churches. Glory is about emperors, generals, presidents, popes, priests, and pastors. Glory is about diplomas, degrees, certifications, ordinations, elections, and appointments. The spotlight, the limelight, the glory shines on those who take up residence on the stages of this world.

But in God's kingdom, in His community, glory is a different kind of light. The Light of the world, Jesus Christ, shines on everyone and everything. Glory isn't reserved for those in power. It isn't reserved for those who run the civil and religious institutions of earth.

God's glory, His light, exposes us all. It shows everyone for who they are. It judges. God's light highlights those in the shadows and brings their good works to light. His light turns up the heat on sin and provides warmth to those who are cold—those who have been left out, abused, kicked aside.

Those who live in His kingdom don't seek glory, nor do they glorify other human beings. They are graciously glorified—enlightened, immersed in beams of brightness—by Jesus.

Every Christmas season my parents place all the cards they receive in a basket. I look forward to reading the annual autobiographies collected there. I usually fix a warm cup of cocoa, grab a comfortable chair surrounded by holiday decorations, and sit down to read beautiful Christmas tales.

One year, I was startled to find that a couple of longtime family friends had written not one, but *two* notes—the first penned by the husband, and the second by the wife.

Letter one:

> WOW!! What a difference two years makes. At this time in 2004, I was writing our annual "Stanton* Family Christmas Letter." Indeed, later that month, Kathy and her entire family had a joyous reunion in our home in Colorado. All was going well, right? WRONG!!
>
> How Joyce and I met is a long story, but suffice it to say it was truly "love at first sight" for both of us, something neither of us expected nor had experienced previously. Now, nearly twenty months later,

* I've changed the names of the people in this story.

the magic of our initial meeting remains, though we have been through many hills and valleys in the interim. Both of us realize more than ever before what it takes to make a relationship work. We are now nearly seven months into our marriage and love each other more than ever.

Letter two:

Dear Friends,

It has been a difficult year for me. On August 4, I found out that Steven has been having an affair with a woman he met through a computer chat line. In September, he left me and filed for divorce. I have gone through the worst time of my life. It has been a difficult year. The house was sold. I moved into an apartment. I am hoping to get out of debt and eventually buy a house. The girls are staying with my sister in Texas. I sometimes feel like it's a dream.

What a messy situation. How could they be so bold as to ruin my comfortable Christmas? Is this appropriate? Aren't we supposed to share only pleasant, sanitized, holy stories? Are the lights of Christmas meant to illuminate ordinary sinners? Is the basket of the church designed to hold these kinds of tales? Don't we who follow the Holy Jesus separate ourselves from those who fall from grace and glory?

The basket of Jesus' relationships was full of broken stories, flawed scenarios, smudged and sullied dramas. He hung out with sinners. He built His church with sinners. The light of Jesus provided warm glory for lives falling apart.

Are you living a life of shadows? That won't exclude you from what Jesus is doing in this world.

The kingdom of God as revealed in Jesus is a different kind of place—a country whose citizens differ from those who've accepted the values of this world. Adventism aright, drenched in Christian spirit, chooses peace over violence, modesty over extravagance, service over power. Adventism at its best chooses a church of humility and humanity—one that values every human life.

We live in a world modeled on Babylon—a world that rewards violence and greed and people who seize the limelight. We need a new kingdom, a new regime. We need a King who will put the world to rights.

Adventism at its best has a message that counters this culture. Jesus heals the eyes that have been blinded by what this world considers normal and gifts us with abnormal sight. Now we view guns, gold, and glory through "gospelled" vision.

---

1. Malcolm Bull and Keith Lockhart, *Seeking a Sanctuary: Seventh-day Adventism and the American Dream* (Bloomington, Ind.: Indiana University Press, 1989), xiii, xiv.

2. Buzzle.com.

3. This list comes from the (SIPRI) Military Expenditure Database and is based on military expenditure data for 2009 (in constant 2008 U.S. dollars). Accessed at http://www.sipri.org.

4. Walter Wink, *Engaging the Powers: Discernment and Resistance in a World of Domination* (Minneapolis: Augsburg Press, 1992), location 218 in Kindle books.

Chapter 6
The Great Controversy

The greatest killer this world has seen has a Latin name: *Status Quo*. The American president Ronald Reagan once quipped that the definition of status quo is "the mess we're in." Status quo is what *is,* the way things *are,* the mess we're *in*. Status quo's English name is simply *life.* And *life* commits homicide against every one of us.

Life kills.

Some die young. Some die old. Some die slowly and painfully. Some die in a New York minute, without warning. But *all* die. This is life's conclusion. And we don't like it.

Throughout this book we are asking, What is the purpose and possibility for Adventist Christianity in the twenty-first century? For Adventism to have a purpose, for it to have even the possibility of relevance and meaning, it must have answers to the *big* questions of life.

- Why are people born, and why do they die?
- Where did we come from, and where are we going?
- Why do pleasure and pain exist?
- What is the meaning of all of this?
- What is Adventist Christianity's sweeping story? What is our metanarrative? What is the defining drama in which all of our individual stories find a universal context? What explanation of life does Adventism give?

Adventism's big story has a name: "the great controversy." Its story begins with God.

God exists outside of time and matter. He is eternal and spiritual. He teems with life. He is full of energy. He is powerful. He is creative. He is good. He is pure. He is lovely. He is loving. He is love. He is beauty. He is light.

That last statement is mind-blowing, but true. "God is light; in him there is no darkness at all" (1 John 1:5, NIV).

God—as pure, intense, radiant light—determines to create. So He makes time, matter, height, depth, animals, minerals, and above all, human beings. And since God is light, life, and love, the creatures He makes are filled with light, life, and love. "God said, 'Let there be light.' " "In him was life, and that life was the light of all mankind" (Genesis 1:3; John 1:4, NIV).

A comprehensive assessment of reality says, "Every good and perfect gift is from above, coming down from the Father of the heavenly lights" (James 1:17, NIV). And the grandest of all gifts—God's magnum opus, His masterpiece, His defining sculpture, the apple of His eye—is human beings. "God created human beings in his own image" (Genesis 1:27, NLT). In other words, God's greatest artwork is a kind of self-portrait.

God made human beings to frolic in the light of His creation. To dance in the light. To magnify. To color. To shade. To reflect. To shimmer and shine. To diffuse and divide. To bask and to beam. To bend the light in new and exciting ways. To take fistfuls of this light and use it—as artists. Engineers. Creators. Fruitful multipliers of His creation.

God has invited human beings to participate in an eternity of

light making,
love making,
life making.

This is our story.

Tragedy

Unfortunately, when creation was still new, tragedy struck. An angelic creature named Lucifer ("Light Bearer") didn't like the nature of God's light. He chose darkness instead, and then he convinced much of the created universe that darkness is better than light, envy is better than peace, hate is better than love—and death is better than life. "How you have fallen from heaven, morning star, son of the dawn!" "[Jesus] replied, 'I saw Satan fall like lightning from heaven' " (Isaiah 14:12; Luke 10:18, NIV).

Satan entices human beings to try his way too. So Adam and Eve choose darkness. And their children and their children's children and generation after generation after them choose violence, shame, control, abuse, greed, selfishness, gluttony, absence, shallowness, darkness, twisted truth, and death.

God is light, so the devil's goal is total darkness. This intention is most nearly realized when Jesus, God in human form, comes to this earth and is murdered—nailed to a cross. The death of God. Of this, Scripture says, "From the sixth hour until the ninth hour there was darkness over all the land" (Matthew 27:45, NKJV). The absence of God means total darkness. Evil's ultimate aim. And so we live in the blackness of the night. "The dominion of darkness" (Colossians 1:13, NIV). Lying, cheating, controlling, selfish darkness. And with it comes cancer. And car crashes. And caskets.

Status quo—life as we know it.

But God won't allow His love to be defeated. He has a plan. Ever since the first sin He has promised that He would break into this dark world with a Messiah of light. Patriarchs, prophets, and kings were given hints of what was to come. Through the Jewish prophet Isaiah, God addressed the coming Messiah in words He meant all to hear: "I will also make you a light for the Gentiles, that my salvation may reach to the ends of the earth" (Isaiah 49:6, NIV).

And Jesus was born, and in the temple the old man Simeon, though his eyes were dimmed with the passing of time, had a 20/20 view of what lay before him in the tiny body of Jesus. "My eyes have seen your salvation, which you have prepared in the sight of all nations: a light for revelation to the Gentiles, and the glory of your people Israel" (Luke 2:30–32, NIV).

Light. God's light. Hope. Joy. Redemption. An opportunity to get the grand narrative back on track. And in Jesus, both rich and poor, Jew and Gentile, male and female, old and young, caught a ray of hope, a wavelength of possibility. Jesus, in fact, said with the clarity of a laser beam, "I am the light of the world" (John 9:5, NIV).

Jesus claims to be the Light of the world. Jesus claims to be light. *The* Light. Jesus claims to be God—the Creator back in town to restore, reclaim, re-create, and redeem. Jesus reveals His divine glory on many occasions, but none more mysteriously and powerfully than when His body is morphed into something spectacularly celestial. "There he was transfigured before them. His face shone like the sun, and his clothes became as white as the light" (Matthew 17:2, NIV).

And then, after His death and burial, after the darkness of Friday's cross, the story tells us of an explosion of light emanating from a tomb. The messenger from heaven and the message are unmistakable: "His appearance was like lightning" (Matthew 28:3, NIV).

Light. Life. Love. These three have triumphed.

The last of the darkness

We are in the last of the days of darkness. Post-Jesus, we enter a new era of hope. The day's first rays of light point to the possibility of morning, yet we still live in this land of nighttime. The apostle Paul got it right: "The night is nearly over; the day is almost here" (Romans 13:12, NIV).

We keep looking at the clock, waiting for the darkness to end. The "fullness of time" is something beyond our understanding. We hope for the marvelous *mañana,* when light will be fully restored to the universe and we will once again participate in the grand project of bending, reflecting, and refracting light—the light of God.

Brilliant living. Bathed in the warmth and glow of God. "There will be no more night. They will not need the light of a lamp or the light of the sun, for the Lord God will give them light. And they will reign forever and ever" (Revelation 22:5, NIV).

This is Adventist Christianity's grand story. We must grasp this defining drama if we are to understand the vision of Adventism. There is a great controversy—a macrowar, a showdown of indescribable size and consequence—between light and darkness, between God and Satan. This is the epic battle, the conflict of the ages. Each combatant has a case to make. For each warrior, the battle is personal. And *we* must decide. *We* must choose sides. To which will we commit life and limb and eternal destiny?

What is the issue at stake?

Ellen White, the church's early prophetic voice, wrote a five-volume masterwork titled The Conflict of the Ages series. Five books. Thirty-six hundred pages. This is her rendering of the big story that she has drawn from the Bible and history. The final volume is titled *The Great Controversy Between Christ and Satan.* Here's the very last paragraph of this substantial tome. (Spoiler alert! This is the punch line. The final scene. The conclusion of the story.)

> The great controversy is ended. Sin and sinners are no more. The entire universe is clean. One pulse of harmony and gladness beats through the vast creation. From Him who created all, flow life and light and gladness, throughout the realms of illimitable space. From the minutest atom to the greatest world, all things, animate and inanimate, in their unshadowed beauty and perfect joy, declare that *God is love.*[1]

Adventists believe there are only two fundamental bases for the decisions we make as human beings. One arises from a claim God has made. The other grows out of Satan's direct contradiction of God's claim. For Adventists, these two arguments provide a window into every big—and small—question.

God's argument to human beings: *I love you.*

Satan's argument: *No, God* doesn't *love you.*

Satan's argument, of course, comes in varieties and with various additions: God doesn't exist. God didn't make us. God made us and left us to fend for ourselves. God made us to be puppets. God made us to be slaves. God made us as a divine joke. God made us—and now He treats us horribly.

What evidence undergirds Satan's case?

The status quo. Circumstances. Whatever is true of your life now, no matter how good or bad, how heavenly or hellish. Satan argues that life itself demonstrates that believing God isn't worth what it costs. Those who believe don't have enough. They don't have it easy enough. "Look at your life," Satan says. "Clearly, either God doesn't exist or He hates you."

- "Adam and Eve, God is withholding perfectly good fruit from you. He doesn't love you."
- "Cain, God doesn't love you—He favors your brother Abel."
- "Saul, God doesn't love you—He favors your enemy David."
- "Jezebel, God doesn't love you; He's telling some people to disobey you."
- "Nebuchadnezzar, God doesn't love you; He hasn't given you the whole world."

- "Job, your life is falling apart—proof that God doesn't love you."
- "Woman at the well, God doesn't love five-time divorcées."
- "John the Baptist, if God loved you, you wouldn't be in prison."
- "Mary, the prostitute, God doesn't love you; you're all used up."
- "Zacchaeus, God doesn't love you; you're a tax cheat."
- "Blind man, if God loved you, you wouldn't be blind."
- "Deaf man, if God loved you, you wouldn't be deaf."
- "Bent-over woman, if God loved you, you wouldn't be crippled."
- "Herod, God doesn't love you; He has another king in mind."
- "Judas, God doesn't love you; He has different opinions."
- "Peter, God doesn't love you because you keep denying Jesus."

Satan says, "God doesn't love you or you or you or you," and he keeps saying it no matter whether the people he's saying it to are experiencing paradise or purgatory at the moment. Your circumstances *right now* are Satan's argument.

God's argument

What about God's argument? What is it based on?

It was the winter of 1970. Bill Bryan was a young medical officer in Vietnam. His bride, Carolyn, lived just outside of Washington, D.C. She was pregnant. Went into labor prematurely. A son was born on March 16, 1970. Born to die, the doctors said. Condolences. Lieutenant Colonel Bruce LaFollett granted permission for Captain Bryan to return stateside. He sent this letter from Vietnam to the new mother:

> 17 March 1970
>
> My dear Mrs. Bryan—
>
> We all were so sad to hear about the premature birth of your boy, and the probability he will not survive.
>
> You're [*sic*] husband has been a sterling, stabilizing influence to all of us who have had the pleasure of associating with him. When this year is over, maybe we can all get together.
>
> Our sympathies, and our best to you both.
>
> Bruce LaFollett

Well, somehow I didn't die. Why? Why did I live? What's the purpose of my survival?

We say God has a plan for that baby's life, but we don't talk about the other babies who didn't make it. We exclaim that Jesus cured our cold symptoms just in time for the big final exam, while others are dying from cancer. We testify to God's finding the perfect job for us while others remain unemployed. We tell about God's providing for us when others are going hungry.

What if I had died in the hours following my birth? What if I hadn't even made it out of the womb? What if the possibilities within me had never been realized? Are favorable circumstances and a decent outcome evidence of God's favor? Are tough times and harsh circumstances indications God doesn't care much about us? How do we interpret our stories?

Here's what God says about His human creatures:

- "Before I formed you in the womb I knew you, before you were born I set you apart" (Jeremiah 1:5, NIV).
- God "chose us in [Jesus] before the creation of the world" (Ephesians 1:4, NIV).
- "You are a chosen people, . . . God's special possession, that you may declare the praises of him who called you out of darkness into his wonderful light" (1 Peter 2:9, NIV).

Jeremiah reveals that God told him He chose him before he was conceived—and God has no favorites; He has plans for us too. Paul says God chose us before matter was created.

And Peter says God chose us, He called us forth, when everything was darkness. That is *before* Genesis 1:1, for it was *before* Creation that all the world was dark. (The first thing God created was light.)

God had you fully in His mind and heart before *anything* was created. He made up His mind to create you long ago. Every life was planned in *His* brain. Lives lived long on this earth. Lives cut off midstream. Lives short lived beyond the womb. Lives ended before birth.

Did you ever wonder whether you would have existed if your parents had married other people? The answer is Yes, for God determined your creation, your existence, your life, *before the creation of the world*. The root of life, the substance of life, began long ago and continues into infinity for those who are in the brain and body of Jesus Christ. "What great love the Father has lavished on us, that we should be called children of God" (1 John 3:1, NIV)!

We are wanted. We are desirable. We are beloved.

The challenge

However, we do face a challenge: the status quo. The present circumstances won't just go away. Life *is* hard. Death continues. So, prove it to us, God! Why should we believe Your claim, Your argument?

Remember this assessment of reality: "The night is nearly over; the day is almost here" (Romans 13:12). How does Saul of Tarsus, the Christian apostle Paul, maintain the hope one must have to write these words? How does he maintain faith in the Advent Hope? How does he—despite the "thorn" that won't go away, despite the beatings and the death threats—maintain such conviction, such hope, such belief, such trust in the love of God?

He has been *enlightened.*

In Acts 9 we see this same Paul filled with hate. He's "breathing out murderous threats" (Acts 9:1, NIV). He's a devoted religious man consumed with killing. He's living in pitch-black darkness. Even though he's a very religious person, he's listening to Satan. But then, while walking down a road, he experiences the enlightenment. "I saw a light from heaven, brighter than the sun, blazing around me" (Acts 26:13, NIV). Paul sees Jesus. He hears Jesus' voice. He feels the heat of Jesus. He touches the *heart* of Jesus. He sees the light. He becomes enlightened. And his encounter with Jesus transforms his life (see verses 13–19).

Paul later writes: "What we preach is not ourselves, but Jesus Christ as Lord, and ourselves as your servants for Jesus' sake. For God, who said, 'Let light shine out of darkness,' made his light shine in our hearts to give us the light of the knowledge of God's glory displayed in the face of Christ" (2 Corinthians 4:5, 6, NIV).

The face of Christ.

The face of Jesus is God's ultimate argument. *Jesus* is God's argument in the great controversy. In the face of Jesus we see the face of God. We see the face of One who desired us in the darkness before creation. We see the face of One who suffered and died just thirty-three years into His sojourn on earth. We see a face of grace, of desire, of love. In Jesus we discover reason to believe that God exists, that He is our Father, that He is a good Father, and that He intends us to have a bright future.

The status quo. Circumstances or Jesus—which will prevail in your life?

As the old hymn says:

Turn your eyes upon Jesus,
Look full in His wonderful face.
And the things of earth will grow strangely dim
In the light of His glory and grace.

Adventism's story is the great controversy. The issue: God's love. God's argument: the face of Jesus. Adventism aright keeps putting forward the face of Jesus.

---

1. Ellen G. White, *The Great Controversy Between Christ and Satan* (Mountain View, Calif.: Pacific Press®, 1950), 678; emphasis added.

Chapter 7
Human Bodies

Imagine that you've just moved to a part of the country you've never visited before. There's a church just down the street from your house, and you decide you'll drop in so you can meet some of your new neighbors.

When you open the front door of the church, a greeter shakes your hand and says, "Welcome to our church! We want you to know that one of our important theological beliefs and behavior expectations is that no member of our church is allowed to have sex at any time. That's true for all married members as well as for those who aren't married. Sexual activity is immoral and is not of God, and the members of our church have committed to pursue only what is spiritual. We invite you to join our congregation."

And suppose the next weekend you visit another church. In this one the greeter welcomes you and then says, "We want you to know that one of our important doctrinal teachings is that all men and women are free to—and in fact, encouraged to—engage in sexual activity throughout our community. We call it 'complex marriage.' Many husbands, many wives!"

The first church reflects the beliefs of the Shakers, an American Christian denomination—one formed in the mid-eighteenth century, and the second one reflects the beliefs of the Oneida Community, a Christian denomination born in mid-nineteenth-century America.

Sexual activity totally restricted?

Sexual activity largely unrestricted?

Should we try to control our bodies by placing them in solitary confinement? Or should we let them run free—without rule, regulation, or any sort of control?

The Christian church has often had an uneasy relationship with sexuality. More broadly, and even more fundamentally, Christians have experienced an awkward relationship with the human body.

"God and Body" is not a comfortable topic for many Christians, so this chapter may bring some discomfort. But we can't appreciate the purpose and possibility of Adventist Christianity without talking about our skin. We can't talk about Adventism without talking about our bodies. Flesh has been the focus of much thought and action in Adventist history. And for good or ill, flesh will be a focus in our future.

A little preview of the pages ahead. First, we'll celebrate one facet of Adventism's relationship with the human body where I believe we've been historically strong—but where we may be becoming weak. *Hint: think auto maintenance.*

Second, I want to challenge Adventism in an area where we have been somewhat weak—but have the capacity to excel. *Hint: think travel.*

Where we came from

Adventism was born in the 1840s, an era when Americans had very poor health. The average lifespan was thirty to forty years. People had little understanding of nutrition. High-fat, high-cholesterol, high-sugar, heavily spiced foods comprised a large portion of the diet of most people. The use of tobacco and alcohol was widespread. Few people were aware of the value of exercise, clean air and water, and moderate exposure to sunshine. Medical advice and procedures often did more harm than good. Hospitals were dangerous places filled with viruses and bacteria. Bloodletting and amputations often led to death. Even much of the clothing of the day threatened people's health. For instance, the long dresses women wore collected filth, such as horse excrement, from the streets and carried it into people's houses—including their kitchens and dining rooms. And the snugness and substantial weight of women's clothing actually impeded the circulation of the blood.

Bathing was uncommon. Toilets were few and far between. Sanitary conditions were a serious public health problem—especially in the cities. In fact, in 1855, the

629,904 people who lived in New York City had just 1,361 bathtubs and 10,388 toilets with which to take care of their needs. That's just one toilet per sixty-one people, and one bathtub per 462 people.[1] The historian George Knight observes, "In 1872 when Ellen White recommended that 'persons in health' should 'bathe as often as twice a week' (3T 70), she was on the cutting edge."[2]

Early Adventists, including Ellen White, were on the cutting edge!

Ellen White—who drew from her interactions with other health reformers of her day and from insights acquired through reflection upon God's Word as well as from the Holy Spirit's instruction—was ahead of her day. In books such as *The Ministry of Healing,* she describes an approach to caring for the human body that has stood up extraordinarily well to the passage of time. Today, articles on health in the periodicals on magazine racks across America trumpet the value of fruits, vegetables, and the generous consumption of water; and the dangers of saturated fat, red meat, alcohol, and cigarettes aren't seriously disputed.

Countless plans for healthy living are available to us, and there is little argument on what the basics are. In addition to the diet outlined above, every reputable healthcare provider recommends exercise—and more than forty-five million people are now members of health clubs. The importance of good sleep, sunshine, the great outdoors, clean air, healthy relationships, a positive attitude, and a pace of life slowed by "sabbaths" are also settled matters these days.[3]

Not so 150 years ago. Not so even 100 years ago. Early Adventists were ahead of their time. Ellen White's approach to medicine and the human body was, astonishingly and convincingly, prophetic. She was, for instance, among the forward-thinking people who spoke against American football. Why? This statistic reveals the reason: in 1905, eighteen college students suffered fatal injuries while playing football. *Eighteen men—boys, really—were killed playing college football in just one season!* And serious concussions were part of almost every game. That's why Ellen White was concerned—she cared about the condition of the human brain.

Today, you can't watch a football game without hearing the commentators express concern for the human head. There is now, even among athletes, coaches, and the business of big-time sports, support for stricter rules concerning helmet-to-helmet collisions. Advocacy for better helmets is widespread. Even comedians have picked up the topic. Jerry Seinfeld had a popular routine in which he pondered the implications of sports helmets, wondering whether a brain that's willing to participate in an activity that requires a helmet is a brain worth protecting in the first place![4]

Think of it: Ellen White was saying in the 1890s what Jerry Seinfeld was joking about in the 1990s!

The point is this: Adventist Christianity can be proud—

not prideful, but proud—that our history is marked by cutting-edge care for the human body. We should appreciate and celebrate the fact that our denomination has built sanitariums and world-class hospitals around the world. Adventists have trained physicians and dentists, nurses and physical therapists, experts in nutrition and exercise, and other healthcare professionals. Adventists have invested in helping people gain freedom from addiction to drugs, alcohol, and tobacco. Physical education has been taught and emphasized at every level of the denomination's school system—from preschool through postgraduate education. The church should celebrate its unwavering commitment to helping people around the world care for their bodies. Clean water. Ample food. Medicine. Sanitary conditions.

We should also celebrate a commitment to purity in sexual behavior—to a kind of sexual living that honors the body as God's temple, His dwelling place, rather than as a piece of meat devoid of human dignity. *Adventists have said that human matter matters. It's valuable.*

Adventists at our best have viewed the "health message" as a word of hope and respect to every human being. Adventists at our best have cared for flesh and blood. We have respected men and women enough to share good information. We have offered gracious help—without guilt, shame, legalism, or manipulative control—in matters of health. Adventists at our best have cared for humanity with considerable patience, world-class expertise, and committed love.

Our emphasis on healthy living has been a tremendous strength for us Adventists. The value of human health has been, well, healthy. But the denomination, at least in America, now exists in a dangerous era—one in which the health message may become sick.

My four worries

I have four worries.

First, what Adventists have to say about health is *no longer unique;* it doesn't belong to us alone. Knowledge about healthy living is widespread. Widely practiced, not always; widely understood, yes. We must be sure that we don't lose interest in caring for our human bodies simply because the message is now common knowledge rather than cutting edge.

I suspect that at times Adventists have been excited about Adventism because it was unique and held special truths no one else had. In many matters—among them the Sabbath, the Second Coming, heaven, hell, and the character of God—this is no longer the case. Many people in the larger Christian community now embrace many things "Adventist." We can't trademark nor copyright the health message. It is firmly in the public domain. We have to beware lest we lose our enthusiasm because others have joined our party.

Second, we must understand that there are *fresh issues* at stake now. We must have something to say beyond "don't eat fried food." For example, we live in an age when body image is a real issue. An obsession with physical appearance has seriously distorted people's perspective on health. What we eat and don't eat, how much we exercise, what we weigh—some of us have become concerned with these matters for the wrong reasons. We're tempted to focus on them because of their effect on our appearance rather than on basic health.

To keep the health message relevant, we may need to argue for *less* focus on the human body. At one time, some people tried to ignore their bodies. Now, there are some who can't stop thinking about their bodies. Now, worship of the body can be a serious problem—spiritually, mentally, and, ironically, physically. How can we best help a generation addicted to a damaged view of "healthy" living?

Another example. We live in an age when technology allows us to become increasingly sedentary and socially isolated. We live in a time of constant stress, toxic anxiety, the acceleration of unrealistic work expectations, and an unrelentingly intense life. Mental and emotional health issues are now talked about more freely than ever before.

Are we engaged in these contemporary health issues?

And how could we miss this next one? We live at a time when perhaps the biggest healthcare crisis America faces is that of funding it. Our society can't afford its crushing cost. Will Adventists lead the way in dealing with this issue? Will we have a role to play? Will we have something to say? Will we participate in a solution? Do we care about the access sons and daughters of God have to life-changing and life-saving medicine?

Bottom line: will Adventists have a physical-education sermon for the twenty-first century? Will the health message be present truth?

Third, someone told me that when an Adventist hospital decided recently to serve only vegetarian dishes in its cafeteria, the *Adventist employees* protested, while those who weren't Adventist celebrated the change! They appreciated the opportunity to eat what they understood to be a healthier diet.

Whether or not that story is true, it seems to me that American culture is moving toward healthy living while Adventist culture—at least in part—is moving away from it. A surefire way to lose the health message is to have less interest in it than society at large has.

Fourth, Adventism is in danger of losing its appreciation for science. Ellen White held great respect for doctrine, for high-quality theology, for those who handled God's Word well. She also desired, and argued for, an Adventist Christianity committed to world-class medicine. She envisioned a church that included, and appreciated, scientific knowledge. She led the church to build institutions of higher learning—including health education—that were well regarded, fully accredited; that were, to quote Dr. Luke, gaining "favor with God and mankind." Biological and other sciences have increased our understanding of disease and its cure. We know a lot more than Adventists knew in the 1800s. Medical science has advanced the cause of human health. Science is not the enemy, but the friend, of the church.

Meant to be used—and enjoyed

At the beginning of this chapter, I mentioned that one of Adventism's strengths has been its understanding of and care for the human body. I hope we won't lose this strength. But, I believe, we may be weak in a related area. Let's return to the metaphor I used early in this chapter: cars.

Automobiles should be clean and well maintained. We should give them good fuel, fresh oil, and other quality lubricants. Regular maintenance is essential to ensuring long life and high performance. But we don't purchase cars to occupy ourselves with maintaining them. They don't exist so we'll have a place to put gas. The purpose cars serve is not to be washed or to be parked in a garage. Mentally stable people don't pay twenty thousand dollars for a car so they can change the belts and spark plugs. People buy cars so they can drive them. Vacations, picnics, adventures, work, ball games, worship services, school, shopping, trips to visit relatives and friends. Cars exist to go places!

Similarly, our bodies don't exist just to eat carrots, avoid cigars and vodka, run the treadmill, and go to bed early. Their purpose isn't simply to be something we can use to prove that we are able to maintain things well—that we're responsible and obedient. The reason God has given us bodies is so we can enjoy them—and worship Him in the process.

Adventism has, in my view, fallen short in celebrating the body as holy, as good, as something to *enjoy*. We have been suspicious of our skin.

Why?

In part, because we have swallowed a piece of the pill manufactured by the Greeks and especially by Plato. He believed that the *spirit* was good but the *body* was evil. From that perspective, then, salvation involves becoming free of the body. So, thanks to its partial embrace of Platonic thinking, much of Christianity has struggled with its view of the human body for a millennium and a half.

Lauren Winner, a historian of religion at Duke University, rightly comments on this historical reality in her brilliant book *Real Sex:*

> The Christian story, at its core, has very positive things to say about bodies, but throughout its history the church has sometimes equivocated. We Christians get embarrassed about our bodies. We are not always sure God likes them very much. We are not always sure whether bodies are good or bad.[5]

Here's a second factor—an interesting footnote from our opening comparison of the Oneida Community and the

Shakers: an influential voice in each group shaped its extreme view of sexuality.

Ann Lee, leader of the Shaker movement, lost four babies. Imagine the crushing grief of losing one little one after another . . . after another . . . after another. We can see why the theology she developed might deplore sex. Human flesh—her own body— had caused her unspeakable pain.

Conversely, the Oneida Community's founder, John Humphrey Noyes, struggled mightily, and unsuccessfully, to control his sexuality. He had a kind of sexual addiction. How does a man with godly sensitivities deal with the guilt of sexual sin? Complex marriage. Open marriage. When your body *fails you,* you have to find some way of "dealing."[6]

Discouragement. Disgust. Demoralization. We read about these downers throughout Christian history. Early church fathers thought the body was evil, and so did certain monks, Protestant Reformers, and Puritan leaders in America. Christians have been uncertain what to *feel* about music, dance, paintings, sculpture, what we see, hear or taste—what we experience in our bodies.[7] We have equated sin with pleasure and pleasure with sin. We have misquoted Jesus' words to the sexually immoral woman, "Go, and sin no more"—too often saying instead to one another, "Go, and have fun with your body no more."

We have attacked the human body rather than sin. We have forgotten those defining words in the Bible's first book:

"And God created stuff. . . . And He created even really, really great stuff . . . the human body. And God said that it was good."

The human body is good. It was made to be enjoyed. The five senses provide five billion *holy* ways to discover pleasure. And this is God's creative will.

Endorphin-rich pleasure

I have loved riding my bicycle for many years. (I'm pretty sure it's not a sin.)

Cycling has caused me a lot of pain. Burning lungs, burning legs, moments when I wanted to scream in anguish. But when I'm riding faithfully, it's the kind of pain that produces a kind of endorphin-rich pleasure that is heavenly.

I used to ride a route called Three Gap in the north Georgia mountains—part of the Tour-de-Georgia, which Lance Armstrong raced for several years. The road was painted with all kinds of colorful things: "Go, Lance, Go!" and international flags, and exhortations in many languages to ride faster. I would crank those pedals up severe inclines and race back down. And after a good, long ride, I was thrashed. My body was spent. But for several days after the ride, I experienced a rich bodily peace. My body simply felt *good.*

Human flesh enjoyed.

I've also experienced the unique tie between physical exercise and human relationships: my wife and I pedaled across Oregon a few summers ago—from the Snake River bordering Idaho to the Pacific Ocean. Physically demanding. Incredible, mountainous beauty. Rich conversation. A compelling marital journey. There's something about physical exercise in community.

Again, from Lauren Winner:

> One might hope that the strongest predictor of teenage virginity would be church involvement—but it's not. A recent study of teenage girls shows that the strongest predictor is actually participation in teenage sports. The girl who plays lacrosse or soccer is more likely to remain chaste than the girl who attends church and youth group. Apparently, sports leagues are doing something right, and the church is (so to speak) dropping the ball.[8]

It isn't enough to say don't smoke marijuana, and don't eat pigs, and don't have sex outside of marriage. An Adventist vision of the body must include more than a list of things to do and not to do in order to have low blood pressure and a pure temple. Adventists must have a positive vision of the body enjoyed in community. If we don't, the body will find a way to experience communal engagement that may not be so healthy. We should enjoy our bodies together—in the right way.

And then there's a connection between the human body and God.

I used to ride a twenty-mile loop regularly, often alone. At first, I filled my iPod with all kinds of music—classical, folk, popular, and religious. And I found something quite curious: I started pedaling the bike and swaying it from side to side *in time to the music.* There was this strange connection between the dance of the bike and the melodies and rhythms of the music.

After a while I started leaving the earphones at home and riding in silence. But one never really rides in total silence. Ask any cyclist; they'll tell you: there is a *sound.* There is a quiet rhythm, a dance, a beat, the pedals and wheels singing together, breeze cutting across the earlobes, the rider's heartbeat, muscles expanding and contracting, lungs taking air in and out.

The body and bike as a symphony orchestra.

I hated to stop. To stop hearing God's whisper in my own body; for millions of cells, in concert, telling of His creative work. Wow!

Psalm 150 says that we must praise God with music and with dancing. The making of music and dancing are both explicitly physical acts. Music calls forth our emotions, our feelings. It brings tears to our eyes. It causes our heart to beat slower or faster. Music practically begs that we get our bodies into the game of life. Perhaps this is why musical opinions can cause such tension in the church. And dancing is a physical act, allowing our bodies to move with pleasure in the ways of God.

Cycling and golf, hockey and hiking, running, skiing, tapping one's foot or sometimes one's whole leg to Tchaikovsky, discovering that fresh strawberries with real whipped cream practically overpower the sensory network of one's tongue.

The body.

A vibrant, prevailing, twenty-first-century Adventism must paint a compelling and pleasurable picture of the human body and our experience. We must be well maintained, but we also must be well traveled. Worshiping God with our bodies is about *pleasure* and experiencing physicality. Creationists believe God created human flesh. The body is good. And just to prove it, God came down in the person of Jesus.

In human flesh.

---

1. George Knight, *Ellen White's World: A Fascinating Look at the Times in Which She Lived* (Hagerstown, Md.: Review and Herald®, 1998), 28–41.

2. Ibid., 112; quoting Ellen G. White, *Testimonies for the Church,* 3:70.

3. Deborah A. Wuest, and Jennifer L. Fisette, *Physical Education, Exercise Science, and Sport,* 17th ed. (New York: McGraw-Hill, 2009), 95.

4. Knight, *Ellen White's World,* 132.

5. Lauren Winner, *Real Sex: The Naked Truth About Chastity* (Grand Rapids, Mich.: Brazos Press, 2005), 33.

6. Information about these two religious groups can be found in many places. I first considered their relationship while reading *Religion in America* by Winthrop S. Hudson and John Corrigan (New York:

Macmillan Publishing Company, 1992), 182–185.

7. Winner, *Real Sex,* 35.

8. Ibid., 18, 19.

CHAPTER 8

HOME

HERE WE COME TO the end of this book's query: *Is there a purpose for Adventist Christianity in the twenty-first century?*

I want to state it clearly: I believe the Adventist movement *can* have a bright future, particularly here in North America. But this is a critical time. The challenges are significant. Here are a few major ones.

- America is fast becoming a post-Christian nation. Some data suggest fewer than one in five adults attend a church service on any given weekend, and much data indicates that the way many people define *Christian* has become far *less* than biblical. In other words, even many of those who claim to be Christian, to be theists, to be churchgoers, view the Christian faith very differently than did Jesus Christ and the apostle Paul. No matter how sanguine we may be about the church's future, the evidence, both empirical and anecdotal, is alarming: the church as we know it is in serious trouble.

- America is fast becoming a postdenominational culture. Denominations are creaking under the weight of outdated governance structures and disconnected theological applications. In other words, many churchgoers, including many Adventists, consider denominations to be characterized by a heavy, top-down ecclesiastical structure and the loss of a nimble, Spirit-prompted, present-truth missionary instinct that has us in real trouble. We aren't organized for success. We live in an era in which brand loyalty—to Ford automobiles or General Electric dishwashers or Methodism—is dead. We can't assume loyalty to Adventism against all odds and over and above all circumstances.
- The color of Adventism in America is gray. Our membership is aging; the data suggest about a fifteen-year difference between the mean age of American Adventists and that of Americans in general. There appears to be a serious problem bridging the gap between the generations. Many young adults are thinking much differently about Adventism than their ancestors did. And when the church appears disinterested, irrelevant, or moralistic, many of them simply move on to other spiritual pastures.[1]

These trends do not mean, however, that we are living in a *secular* culture. We actually are living in an exceptionally *spiritual* culture—an age of intense spiritual curiosity and commitment. People are interested in God, Jesus, Buddha, Muhammad, and Moses. Here's the dark twist: while *spiritual* desire is rising, *church* desire is undergoing a stark decline—as the titles of these recent books (among others) illustrate:

- *They Love Jesus, but Not the Church* (by Dan Kimball)
- *Revolution: Finding Vibrant Faith Beyond the Walls of the Church* (by David Kinnamen)
- *Divine Nobodies: Shedding Religion to Find God* (by Jim Palmer)
- *God Without Religion* (by Andrew Farley)

The message is clear: young adults are saying Yes to Jesus, faith, and God, but No to church and religion.

What should the church do? Yell louder? Work harder? Get more creative? Crack down? Leap to the future? Grab hold of the past? Become more technologically savvy? Seek to pump up the remaining faithful with some kind of spiritual steroids?

I believe the answer begins with vision: a theological vision, an ecclesiological vision. We must choose a vision of Adventist Christianity for the future. We must decide how Adventist Christianity will make and remake itself. We must commit ourselves to something more than mere survival strategies—we need bold and beautiful dreams emerging from every generation and locality. We need green-cord dreams. We need the One. We need Jesus.

This book is all about choices. Adventists must make fundamental, foundational choices that will inform our dreams and visions of a denominational future. The fate of American Adventism in the years ahead will be shaped by these choices.

- Will Jesus be *everything* in Adventism? Or will He be a sideshow or merely some part of a supposedly larger whole? (Chapter 1)
- Will Adventism be humble and generous in the way that Jesus was, talking little of itself and building bridges with the rest of the Christian community, or will we boast much about ourselves and the grand significance of our organization—becoming more isolated, puritan, and separatist along the way? (Chapter 2)
- Will we desire the Bible again—as a way to fall in love with Jesus? Will the life and writings of Ellen White inspire within us a greater affection for Scripture, or will we treat her as either demon or deity? Will we find her humanity too much to handle and so either reject her example or grant her the status of being the final arbiter of the Bible? (Chapter 3)

- Will we live for heaven alone, or will we live to create heaven on earth—the prayer-vision of Jesus? Will we be useless dreamers, or will we be awake to meeting the needs of the suffering *Jesus/people** in our world? (Chapter 4)
- Will we crave violence, wealth, and power, or will we humbly choose peace, simplicity, and service? Will we choose the way of human religious powers or the way of Jesus? (Chapter 5)
- Will we get lost in minor theological disputes and church spats, or will we live within the grand story of the great controversy, choosing Jesus instead of the accusations of Satan? (Chapter 6)
- Will we lose our will to maintain healthy bodies and reject the holy pleasure of our five senses, or will we keep and grow an emphasis on clean living, with an increased focus on celebrating the experience of life not simply as spirit, but also as flesh and blood? Will we honor and celebrate our bodies as the body of Christ, as His creation? (Chapter 7)

And now we face one more choice, a final one: What will we think about the end times? What will we, as a movement of people called Adventists, say to our children about the return of Jesus Christ?

---

* Matthew 25:40, "Whatever you did for one of the least of these brothers and sisters of mine, you did for me" (NIV).

Forty years ago, the American folk singer John Denver first sang a nostalgic song that pictures West Virginia as "almost heaven" and calls upon "country roads" to take him "home, to the place I belong." He claims he hears his homeland calling him, and says,

> drivin' down the road I get a feelin'
> That I should have been home yesterday.

Homesickness.

The poet Maya Angelou says *the ache for home lives in all of us.* Have you ever been homesick, felt the ache for home? Was it

- the first time your parents left you with the babysitter?
- in kindergarten? First grade? Summer camp?
- the year you were a student missionary?
- in college?
- at the funeral of a loved one?
- coming upon that picture of him, or her, or them?
- during an unexpected quiet moment that gave birth to a wave of nostalgia?
- when you felt a secret longing to be with someone or to be somewhere . . . an urge that tells you, "I'm not home."

Home is huge.

Don't believe me? Try making a crack about somebody's

hometown or somebody's mother (the person who personifies home). Just try insulting Alabama or California or Ireland. Or Mama. Watch out—home is very near our hearts.

John Denver longed to be taken home, where he belongs, and so do I. And I suspect you do too. We are—all of us—homesick. Homesickness is the great human epidemic. It is the reason people live in dark depression. It is the reason we are cut so deeply at funerals. It is the condition that causes us to fight, to drown our sorrows, to search for meaning, to hope, to dream, to run, to hide, to wonder, to wander, and to wish for something better. Homesickness is the reason we are so incurably insecure.

What is this homesickness? Where does it come from?

Genesis 3 explains how we came to be separated from home. Sin enters the world. Woman and man decide hometown is not all God cracks it up to be, so God grants their wish, their choice, their impulsive desire, and they are locked out of the Garden of Eden, banished from home. Ever since that fateful day, all of us human beings have been separated from our home. Ever since, we have suffered as aliens and strangers. We aren't where we are supposed to be. We can't speak the language of this land. We don't know the customs of this land. This is foreign territory. This land brings infant mortality, teenage suicide, midlife crises, and the loneliness of old age.

This world is not our home.

Even though countless generations of human beings

have lived here, we've failed to develop a resistance to sin, an immunity to death. We haven't adapted to this hostile territory. Single people may long to be married, but marriage isn't home. Married people can long for children, but parenting isn't home. The refugee can long for safe passage back to the soil of familiarity, but that's no longer home either. People can return to the land of their roots—South Carolina, North Dakota, eastern Washington, or even West Virginia, but these places aren't home. Not ultimate home. Not the ultimate answer to our homesickness. They're not Eden.

The only solution to our chronic homesickness is to truly go home. Where is our true home? A carved wood sign in our house says it so powerfully: "Home is where your story begins."

Adventist Christians have said that our story begins with God, in heaven, in Paradise, and then on a perfect earth. Our story begins in the arms of God. Our home is with God. Adventists are aliens, strangers, foreigners. This place is not for us. Not because we are Adventists, but because we are human beings.

How do we get back home?

The Bible describes four passageways from this world to that world, from this foreign earth to the home of heaven. First, the way of Enoch and Elijah, who went to heaven without ever experiencing death. Second, the way of Moses, who died, but now, even before Jesus' return to earth, communes with God. Third, the way of death, of quiet rest, of peaceful sleep in the arms of Jesus until the dead in Christ are awakened by the angelic trumpet. Fourth, the way of end-time existence, of living through the time when this old world is broken apart by the arrival of Jesus Christ and then restored to its original beauty.

Ultimately, these four ways find their power in the only Way, Jesus Christ. Seventh-day Adventists believe that Jesus is coming soon. This movement began with a conviction that human beings are in the final phase of earth's history as a fallen, sin-infected place. Adam and Eve left home plate, and the history of this fallen world has moved forward, rounding first, touching second, crossing third . . . and now, Adventists believe, we're in the home stretch. We're running toward home. Adventists believe that Jesus is coming to take us home any day now.

There are many decisions in life. What are you going to do this summer? What should your major in college be? Should you get married? Whom should you marry? Where should you live? How will you spend your money? What values will you adopt and live in this world? Many decisions. All with consequences—some small; some large. But the biggest decision, bigger than all the rest combined—*the* decision—is whether you will choose heaven. Whether you will choose to go home.

Jesus invites us—invites you: "Do not let your hearts be troubled. You believe in God; believe also in me. My Father's house has many rooms; if that were not so, would I have told you that I am going there to prepare a place for you? And if I go and prepare a place for you, I will come back and take you to be with me that you also may be where I am" (John 14:1–3, NIV).

And then He says, "I am the way."

"I am the pathway."

"I am the country road."

And so we sing, "Take me home *now,* country road. Take me home *now,* Jesus—to the place I belong." The primal impulse of Adventism is to go home, to be with Jesus.

We Adventists have a choice: we can fixate on end-time speculations. We can spend time, treasure, and parchment scaring people about the speeches of presidents, the lectures of prime ministers, the pontifications of popes. We can worry about future times of trouble while the majority of the people in this world live in times of trouble now. We can speculate. We can alarm. We can predict. We can focus on time, and times. We can try to get God to change His timing by means of our own self-righteousness. We can stay on edge and keep one another on edge. Or we can be, or increasingly become, a movement of people who simply want to go home and who want to help others understand their deep, persistent homesickness.

We can be a people of hope and home.

Dust-dry twenty-first-century Adventists can immerse themselves in the teardrops of the Great Disappointment.

We can cultivate a simple, primal, powerful, foundational longing to be with Jesus. We can bathe ourselves and our denomination in a deep, insatiable desire to be with Jesus, who is

HOME!

1. For a fuller treatment of these issues, see my article "Tomorrow," first published in *Adventist Today* and now posted at www.breakfastfires.blogspot.com.

PRAISE FOR *THE GREEN CORD DREAM*

Alex Bryan captures the essence of Adventism in broad strokes that draw us all to Jesus. He raises the questions that people ask only in the privacy of their homes, and he seeks the answers in our Lord. Join Alex on his journey as he finds hope for the present and life for the future of our movement.

Japhet De Oliveira
Director, Center for Youth Evangelism
Andrews University

Alex embraces his church with a vibrant and affectionate passion. He clearly sees Jesus as the soul and lifeblood of Adventism, and his desire for this denomination to find a path to a vital, relevant, and thriving future is clear. This book is as refreshing as it is inspirational.

Tami Cinquemani
Worship Director
Florida Hospital Church

Pastor Bryan brings a fresh view of the centrality of Jesus in Adventist roots that challenges twenty-first-century readers to see whether Jesus is truly ALL in their lives. His personal stories are engaging, and his dialogue relevant. A refreshing read, this book directs our focus back on the One of our church.

Brandy Kirstein
Collegedale, Tennessee

Alex Bryan gets it. This Jesus-drenched piece is a breath of fresh air. Alex has distilled what it means to be a historic, primal, and elemental Adventist. He has taken the chaff off the wheat and has given us the life-giving Bread: Jesus. All. Alex has mined history, culture, and the themes of Adventism, and he rightly finds Jesus in the midst of all of these. Read this book to reorient, reapply, and restructure your relationship with Jesus as seen through the Adventist experience.

Timothy Gillespie
Young Adult Pastor
Loma Linda University Church